BREAKING CHAINS THROUGH THE POWER OF CHRIST JESUS

Diane M. Neumann

ISBN: 9798450572147

INTRODUCTION

I Peter 2:9

"But you are a chosen people, a royal priesthood, a holy nation, a people belonging to God, that you may declare the praises of Him who called you out of darkness into the wondrous light."

We who choose to believe Jesus Christ as Savior and Lord, acknowledge Him as part of the Triune God. We believe Jesus Christ obeyed His Father God's will, accepting the role of innocent sacrifice for payment for all people's sins for all time and in all places. We call ourselves Christians. We acknowledge Jesus's death by crucifixion and His rising again as a whole person through the power of the Holy Spirit. For these people, this book is written.

Jesus stated that He came to free the captives, to heal the broken hearted, and release the prisoners of darkness. Many of us who have accepted Jesus as Lord are still caught in wrong thinking, blaming ourselves for events that God has already forgiven, and caught under self-condemnation, unearned guilt, and shame. This is not the intent of our God. We have not accepted the full benefits Jesus created when He overcame the enemy and captured all power and authority on earth and under the earth. God awarded Jesus this at His resurrection. I formerly walked this path of crippling myself with wrong thinking and accepting blame when God did not see any. I learned how to embrace Jesus' promises and righteousness. I entered into a fuller relationship with Christ. I invite you to examine what the Holy Spirit has given me to share with you. We are of the Light, the true light that shines in the darkness and the darkness cannot overcome it.

In God's eyes we are the righteousness of Christ. We live in a new covenant of grace and truth. There is freedom and joy in this life. Accept the full power and authority of Jesus as children of God, wholly acceptable to God. Begin to know that nothing you do or say can separate you from the love of God. Walk in His protection and love, glorifying our God.

This book is dedicated to the Glory of God as revealed by Jesus Christ's life and death and resurrection. It is through the help of the Holy Spirit I have taken my journey. The Holy Spirit's thoughts and directions have guided my hand as I write these chapters. Praise be to God!

TABLE OF CONTENTS

1

The Ultimate Mystery

The Creator of the universe wants a personal, loving relationship with His creation, humanity. It is amazing that God wants to directly talk His people. God loves His people and seeks to give them gifts. If people are honest with themselves, they see many unlovable parts within themselves. People remember times, when growing up, they wanted something so badly they cheated or lied or remained silent to achieve what they wanted. In this mindset people overlooked selfishness, defending themselves, claiming the want justified the actions. The mere habit of justifying demonstrates a sense of wrong. Now add to this fact that an all-knowing God, who can read each heart and mind wants a relationship with people. Wow!

Deep down there is a part of humanity that states, "This makes no sense. Why would God, Creator of everything, balancer of all things, source of truth, justice, and mercy want a relationship with a messed-up person like me?" There is no answer to the why, thus, the mystery. The better question is, "what does a person do about the information that God is searching your heart and mind as He seeks to relate to you?"

Some people choose to ignore God. They pretend God did not create everything. Rather, they claim that creation happened as a lucky accident, of the right stuff being hit by lightning at just the right time. Poof! Life happened. Then life is a happy accident, there is no god, and people can ignore their conscience, and do as they will. These are called evolutionists. Others are uncomfortable with the happy accident theory and ascribe creation to a Creator that has better things to do than hang around with His creation. They believe God is out there somewhere doing God things, leaving His people on their own to muddle through life. Since the majority of these believers have a sense of conscience, their beliefs include something about doing good works to help others, not being too selfish, yet still seeking a self-satisfying lifestyle.

For those people who answer, "I am going to try a have a relationship with God, and discover what He wants with me," they search. For Christians, the answers are in the Bible for the question, "Now how do I build a relationship with God?" Just as one begins to read and understand the Bible, God throws another curve ball right at a person's brain. Not only does God seek to have a relationship with His people, but God knows His people are not very good at keeping faith with God, trusting God, and carrying our end of the relationship by honoring God. Being out of favor with God and not following the rules He wrote is called sin. So, this All-Powerful Being, seeing how inept His people were at being in a healthy relationship with God, sent His son, Jesus Christ, to take the punishment one time, for all people, for everyone's sins no matter where they live, or when they were born. Jesus stated on the cross, "It is finished." His sacrifice was total. Now all sins are covered by His blood and His death. Christians also know Jesus Christ rose from the dead and lives eternally. Some may be thinking there has to be a gimmick in this gift.

Well, there is. God wants individuals to accept Jesus Christ as their Savior and acknowledge Him as Lord. Accepting Jesus as Lord means surrendering the power over one's life. It means no longer asserting an individual's way and will, but whatever God's will is for each person. After that, His people are in a relationship with God, clear and free of any punishment, guilt, or consequences for messing up the relationship with God. It is a start over card in life and relationship with God. God is faithful to His words and promises. Once people accept Jesus as Savior and Lord of their life, individuals have salvation and eternal life with God.

One may ask why God did this, and the answer is still the same. God wants a healthy relationship with people, period. God knows His people so well that the second ultimate mystery is patterned after the first. He loves us. John 3:16–18:

"16For God so loved the world that he gave His one and only Son, that whoever believes in him shall not perish but have eternal life. 17For God did not send His Son to condemn the world, but to save the world through Him. Whoever believes in Him is not condemned. 18But whoever does not believe stands condemned already because he has not believed in the name of God's one and only Son."

Thus, humanity get a pass, "out of condemnation" card. The card must be activated by each individual in order to be used. Remember, it costs a person something. The cost is a life truly surrendered to God. Further studying of the Bible shows one how to relate to God. Within Jesus' words, people find God sent His Holy Spirit to be a comforter, a teacher, and interpreter of the Bible. The third mystery is His people have help available. Just as soon as His people state, "I don't understand what I am reading," or "I'm not very good at understanding the Bible," God's third part of Himself, the Holy Spirit intercedes. The Holy spirit was sent to God's people to be a part of them when they accepted Jesus as Lord. This Holy Spirit is an interpreter, a counselor, an advocate, and a teacher, so that each person may have a personal relationship with God.

After one has accepted Jesus as one's Savior, the Son of God and the free gift of salvation, and carry the Holy Spirit inside of them, then another concern hits the brain. The question is: "How do I have a relationship with a God who has forgiven me all my mistakes, bad attitudes, and selfish acts? If I couldn't be good before being forgiven, how am I supposed to act now?"

If you need the Cliff Notes version of how to be in relationship with God, know the answer Jesus gave to the Pharisees. When the Pharisees asked Jesus, what was the greatest law, Jesus said in Matthew 22:37-39,

[37]Jesus said, "Love the Lord your God with all your heart, and with all your soul and all your mind. [38]This is the first and greatest commandment. [93]And the second is like it: Love your neighbor as yourself. All the law and prophets hang on these two commandments."

This is the crux of humanity's relationship with God. Notice it starts with a love relationship. When people are grateful for what God has done for them, through Jesus Christ, they stand in awe and their hearts open to the possibility of returning this amazing love. To be grateful, one needs to embrace all the selfish actions, thoughts and emotions that caused strife with others. Accept responsibility for them, and then give them up onto the cross of Jesus. Ownership of these things leads to understanding of the source of people's dissatisfaction in life. These are the source of pain, regret, blame and shame. Doing life in a selfish mode does not give lasting peace or joy. Giving them over to Jesus, when His people accept Him as Lord, releases such pressure in their lives. Gratitude arises in a person's soul.

Christians call this process grace. Simply, grace is a gift each person receives from God that was not deserved or earned. His people receive the best present ever and did nothing to earn it. As a matter of fact, it cannot be earned since it is a love gift from God. Like the first love in our lives, people stumble through, trying to return this love. They are awkward when talking to God, not knowing what to say. People want to give something back to God, serve in some way. At the beginning level, they are not into the relationship long enough to know what they can offer.

Some are embarrassed about themselves and their former life, so they cover up parts that they see as unacceptable. If they keep talking to God, they find nothing they do as works is acceptable to reimburse God for the gift. As long as they have accepted responsibility for behaviors, attitudes and emotions that were outside of God's order and laws, everything is covered by the blood of Jesus in His sacrifice on the cross. His people are on a journey to develop a long-lasting relationship. One may ask, "but what if I remember something I did in the past and didn't own it when I accepted Jesus as Lord and Master of my Life?" Relax. Just return in prayer to God and own it, asking for forgiveness and healing. In fact, Jesus' payment is ongoing. No longer are His people under the old covenant of laws and punishment. When God looks at His people, He sees Jesus and they stand righteous in His presence. This fact is what is called amazing love or God's mercy.

Many people have a hard time getting their brains to accept this unconditional, total love. Some people are still looking to be punished. They have only known conditional love. In conditional love, when one displeases the other person, there is punishment. Even the mistakes one makes after entering in relationship with God are covered by the blood of Jesus when a person admits transgressions and asks forgiveness. Sometimes His people "mess up," and slip back into old habits. How they handle the slip up affects their relationship with God. In a two way, mutually respectful relationship, if one person realizes one's actions have hurt the other person in some way, it is the first person's responsibility to make peace and clear the differences that might grow. Admitting guilt on the first person's part is the first step. Asking for forgiveness and moving back into fellowship is what God wants. It simply means saying, "I'm sorry God I messed up. I tried but I need your help. Help me lean on you more and myself less." See, even the sins committed after one has accepted Jesus are covered by Jesus' blood. His people are seen as righteous. God is not surprised when His people slip.

God has dealt with humanity for a long time and knows their tendencies. He knows the enemy that tries to pull them away from God. Almighty God looks into and knows people's hearts. He loves His people despite their imperfections. It is the relationship that matters, not the sin. It is the sincere heart seeking a relationship with God that shines through the confession of guilt and the desire to be in right relationship with God. As in any healthy relationship, admit the wrong and ask for help not to not do it again. One of Jesus' apostles describes it this way. I John 1:9:

"If we confess our sins, he is faithful and just and will forgive us our sins and purify us from all unrighteousness."

But sometimes pride is too much. Sometimes His people are so uncomfortable with being honest with God, they want to end the relationship. Being vulnerable means God knows everything in a person's heart and mind. Some people want to live in denial, not admitting their selfish part in events that occur. A God who knows truth destroys this denial. When people, willing with conscious mind and purpose, choose to do their own will, rather than remain in God's will, they are in disobedience. Proverbs 28:13-14:

"[13]Whoever conceals their sins does not prosper, but one who confesses and renounces them finds mercy. [14]Blessed is the one who always trembles before God, but whoever hardens their heart falls into trouble."

By choosing self-will over God's will and consciously ignoring God, His people are not in harmony with God's purpose, the love relationship with God, and God's plan for humanity. Eventually that willful spiritual disobedience can become a habit in people's souls. This habit can become so embedded that it eventually resides in their physical bodies. This is disease: not being in harmony with God. Please note this is not a punishment from God, but rather a result of our own choosing. As stated in James 1:13–15,

"¹³When tempted, no one should say, "God is tempting me." For God cannot be tempted by evil, nor does he tempt anyone; ¹⁴ but each person is tempted when they are dragged away by their own evil desire and enticed. ¹⁵ Then, after desire has conceived, it gives birth to sin; and sin, when it is full-grown, gives birth to death."

When Christians choose to stay in relationship with God, admitting individual slip ups of returning to old habits and talking to God about it, God comes running to embrace them, joyful over their return. God's nature is to be merciful. The parable of the prodigal son shows the father, the symbol for God, seeing the lost son. The father runs to greet his son, not even allowing the son to debase himself, but rather throwing a party for his return. God's mercy is choosing to withhold punishment and to show compassion and forgiveness towards someone whom God has the power to judge and punish. It is God's nature to be merciful and His choice. How is this possible? It is possible through the act of Jesus, God's Son taking on every sin ever committed unto Himself on the cross and God claiming it is a fair exchange to meet the justice of

God's laws. Sin is choosing to be outside of the balance Creator God placed in His creation to keep all things in harmony. Sin is rebellion to the order. It produces chaos, and self-centered focus. Now, when God sees someone who has accepted Jesus as Lord, God sees someone in righteous standing with Him. In the new relationship, like in any love relationship, one person admitting he or she has been self-centered, ignored the needs of the other, reconciles the relationship. Punishment and rules of behavior are not part of a loving relationship when people give their whole self, mind, will, and heart to God. To love God with a whole heart is a process, not simply an action. As in any love relationship, through actions, people learn about their beloved as well as themselves. Daily interactions of meeting the desires of the beloved builds the relationship. Daily communication recognizes each person's part in the relationship with the beloved. As both participate at this level, it clarifies the love relationship. Reconciliation and forgiveness are learned processes in this love relationship.

Thus, there are two steps in a renewed relationship with God. The first is achieved by accepting Jesus Christ's atonement for a person's sins by claiming Jesus as the Son of God, crucified and raised from the dead. A person is then forgiven sins and in righteous relationship with God. The second step is entering into a daily communication with God.

God is faithful with His promises and covenants and does not walk away. In Romans 8:38-39 it states,

"[38]For I am convinced that neither death nor life, neither angels nor demons, neither the present nor the future, nor powers, [39]neither height nor depth, nor anything else in all creation, will be able to separate us from the love of God that is in Christ Jesus our Lord."

Now these are the words of a man who persecuted, executed, and harassed Christians until Jesus called this man, Paul, to Himself. If someone who carried such a burden of knowing his earlier actions were against God, and now states nothing can separate us from the promise and love of God, how can God's people question God's commitment and love? Yet, there is more to it. In a dynamic love relationship, there is choice. God created humanity with free will. God's people can choose to abandon or cause stress in the relationship. By people's wrong thinking, turning their hearts away from God, or negative attitudes, people can build walls and barriers that limit the relationship.

Looking at the statements Jesus made to the Pharisees again, there are three levels of harmony essential to building a healthy, mutual, and loving relationship with God. There are three levels of responsibility for humanity within the summary of God's law.

1.   Harmony in relationship with God.
2.   Harmony with yourself and knowledge of who you are in Christ Jesus.

3.   Healthy fellowship with others.

When God's people are not in harmony with any of these three areas, they start a downward path that divides them from God, and His divine purpose for humanity. Choosing to be outside of the harmony of God's balanced laws of creation is living in rebellion. It leads to chaos. Chaos destroys life. It eventually leads to death. Continuous willful disobedience or rebellion in any of these three areas over time triggers bodily dysfunction, or what is commonly called disease. This is not punishment from God for rebellion, but natural results from choosing to be outside God's protection and blessing.   Remember, by choosing to accept Jesus as Lord, all of our misbehaviors are forgiven.   By staying in relationship with God and growing in the love for Him, God showers blessings and gifts on His people.   Turning away from the relationship does not deny salvation.   How individuals carry their end of the love relationship, using their whole heart, mind and will to love God is their choice. As stated in Deuteronomy 30:19–20,

"[19]This day I call the heavens and the earth as witnesses against you that I have set before you life and death, blessings and curses. Now choose life, so that you and your children may live [20] and that you may love the LORD your God, listen to his voice, and hold fast to him. For the LORD is your life, and he will give you many years in the land he swore to give to your fathers, Abraham, Isaac and Jacob."

Creation of our bodies by God

God created humanity to possess three related, but different bodies. People are first spiritual beings possessing a spirit body. Unfortunately, modern humanity believes the lie that people are first physical bodies. This lie emphasizes a belief of creation by evolution, which concentrates on molecules (non-living entities). Using an electrical source, created in lightening, somehow lifeless substances are joined together and changed into thinking beings with choice and free will. There are other writers who have shown how impossible this can be! This is backward thinking. God first imagined each person in spirit form, then God molded individuals in their mother's womb to develop a physical body. To these two bodies God added a soul that communicates between the two bodies. Psalms 139:13:

"For you created my inmost being; you knit me together in my mother's womb"

First God created each person's inmost being. The Bible is not describing internal organs, but rather a person's spirit. Then God placed each person in their mother's womb to form a physical body. God took the DNA of the mother and combined it with the father's DNA to form a physical body. Two hundred plus sperms are needed to weaken the outer layer of the ova in order for one to successfully enter and unite. God's hand is even in the choosing of which sperm will unite to create a new body to hold the spirit He has already made.

In Genesis Chapter one, verse two, God states, "the spirit of God was hovering over the water". This is not a physical body, but a spirit. In Genesis 1:26a, our triune God states, *"Let us make man in our image, in our likeness"*.

Humanity is first spirit. Secondly, God is three in one, Father, Son who is Christ Jesus, and Holy Spirit. When God talks to all three parts of Himself, He describes making humanity in three parts, similar to the Godhead. One part is spirit, and the second part is a physical body but there is a third part, a mediator of the other two, a soul.

Biblical texts use a Greek word, "suneidesis" meaning a knowing within or conscience. It is translated from the Hebrew word and referenced in Strong's Exhaustive Concordance as #4893. In Romans 2:15 Paul describes this soul, using the same word, "suneidesis":

"When Gentiles who do not have the Law, do by nature things required by the Law; since they show the requirement of the Law are written on their hearts, their consciences also bear witness and their thoughts now accusing now even defending them."

Paul is acknowledging that all people have a conscience or soul body that influences the choices made in life. Later, in First Thessalonians, Paul blesses the followers of Jesus in this prayer (1 Thessalonians 5: 23):

"May God himself, the God of peace sanctify you through and through. May your whole spirit, soul and body be kept blameless at the coming of our Lord Jesus Christ."

Furthermore, in Romans 9:1-2,

"¹I tell the truth in Christ, I am not lying, my conscience also bearing me witness in the Holy Spirit, ² that I have great sorrow and continual grief in my heart."

Paul states his conscience confirms the truth he is speaking by acknowledging agreement with the Holy Spirit. In this statement, Paul's spirit, and the Holy Spirit, are acknowledged and interpreted through the soul, Paul's conscience. A redeemed human soul does the acknowledging of what the spirit has confirmed through the power of our counselor, The Holy Spirit. It is recorded in 1 Peter 3:16–17,

"¹⁶keeping a clear conscience, so that those who speak maliciously against your good behavior in Christ may be ashamed of their slander. ¹⁷ For it is better, if it is God's will, to suffer for doing good than for doing evil."

Peter addresses the hard questions of staying the course under persecution for doing good. He states to keep a clear conscience ("suneidesis"). Again, Peter is also speaking of the third body, the soul.

In Deuteronomy Chapter 6 verse 5, Israel is admonished to love your God with all your soul. It is the first commandment. To love is a chosen action. It involves the will and decision-making process. Here is a demonstration of what the will center or conscience does. Like the New Testament quotes, the soul is a separate entity within humanity. Thus,

God created humanity with three inter-related bodies: spirit, soul, and physical body.

Though these three bodies, spirit, physical body, and soul have different functions, each is interdependent upon the other. As humanity was made in God's image, this interconnection communicates to each other. What happens in one body effects the other two. This is the mystery of life. Unlike other creatures God created on this earth, humanity is the only one with these three bodies. The core of the difference is a will and conscience, or soul that communicates between the other two.

The believers of evolution attempt to demonstrate the animals have the ability to think and choose since it is essential to their belief system to pull humanity's "willful-thinking-choosing part", the soul, down to the animal instinct level. In their beliefs, humanity is not responsible for the choices they make. In their system, humanity becomes chained to instincts which they cannot control, that are governed by sensual desires. There is no hope to overcome and control desires. In their understanding, when a person tries and fails to control desires, then condemnation follows without hope. Life becomes futile and purposeless. Christian belief states otherwise.

Christians acknowledge the three bodies are united in one person. These bodies affect each other. When people remain in harmony with God, each body functions as God intended.

Disharmony is caused by rebelling from the ordained mandates of creation. Disharmony allows separation from God through a person's own choice. God has provided a way to re-unite with Him in right relationship through Christ Jesus's death and resurrection. By accepting Jesus as Lord and the sacrifice for our rebellion, God's people enter in right relationship again. Harmony occurs not by a person's own actions, but as an individual surrenders one will over to God. It is God's choice to accept Jesus's sacrifice for humanity's willful rebellion. Through God's mercy and grace, humanity is again in unity with God.

SECTION 1
BUILDING WALLS WHICH SEPARATE US FROM GOD

2

Free the Captives

When Isaiah describes the Christ, who is to come, he states in Isaiah 61:1,

"The Spirit of the Sovereign Lord is on me, because the Lord has anointed me to proclaim good news to the poor. He has sent me to bind up the brokenhearted, to proclaim freedom for the captives and release from darkness the prisoners."

Jesus Christ was sent by God with a mission for humanity. When he returned to Nazareth, (his hometown) after his baptism and time in the dessert, he read this passage in the synagogue on the Sabbath as recorded in Luke Chapter 4 verses 16-21. Jesus stated that today that passage has been fulfilled. During Jesus's time walking the earth, he healed all who were brought to him. The statement that the Savior frees the captives and releases from darkness the prisoners, includes physical healing. Sin was considered something that captivated people exhibiting its control in many bodily ailments. People were considered prisoners to the powers of darkness when caught in continual sin and believed this manifested itself in physical illness, or bodily dysfunction and crippling. When the report of Jesus healings of all who were brought to Him reached the multitude, many came to see and receive these miracle healings. Little did they know until after Jesus' death and resurrection, this statement meant so much more.

The good news is for those who are poor in spirit. Since all people are under the burden of rebellion and death, all are poor in spirit. His death and resurrection are good news to all who accept and acknowledge Jesus is Lord and Savior. The Son of God, who knew no sin, became the ultimate sin offering for those who accept Jesus. 2 Corinthians 5:21:

"God made Him who had no sin to be sin for us, so that in him we might become the righteousness of God."

God prepared the Israelites to recognize this process with two major events in their history. When Abraham was commanded to sacrifice his only son, Isaac, God provided an alternative. Abraham was judged righteous in God's sight because he was obedient. The mercy of God provided an alternative, a ram instead of a son was slain (Genesis 22:2–14).

After instituting a new covenant with the Israelites at Mount Sinai, Moses was commanded to provide sin offerings, sacrifices of animals to receive forgiveness of sins (Exodus 20: 24–26). Thus, an understanding grew with practice among the Israelites that something living could be substituted for the sins of others. A third event, Passover, is a time celebrated every year to remember how the Israelites were finally released from Egypt. Every family was commanded to slay a lamb and place the blood over the lintel and sides of the outside door so when the angel of death, who sought the first-born in all households, would pass over those secured in the blood. The lamb was then eaten after being prepared in a specific method (Deuteronomy 16:1-8). On the other side of Jesus' resurrection, Jesus himself re-explained this to His disciples who preached this good news to the poor in spirit. Many Christians are aware that death was conquered at the cross. This was not all that happened at the cross. These are some of what Jesus accomplished at the cross:

> Emotional healing for broken hearted people.
> Disease ruling over physical bodies was broken.
> Freeing people from the bondage of self will.
> Shining truth over the lies of Satan.
> Returning people to their original role God intended on this earth.

2 Corinthians 5:17–19 (RSV) states,

Therefore, if anyone is in Christ, he is a new creation; the old has passed away; behold, the new has come. 18 All this if from God, who through Christ reconciled us to Himself, and gave us the ministry of reconciliation, 19 that is, that in Christ God was reconciling the world to Himself, not counting their trespasses against them, and entrusting to us the message of reconciliation.

Christians are a new creation. When people submit to the offered sacrifice, they no longer have their rebellion held against then. God's people are no longer under the rule of chaos leading to destruction and death. Once reconciled with God, He gave His people another promise, as a result of Jesus' sacrifice.

Notice in 2 Corinthians 5:21,

"God made Him who had no sin to be sin for us, that we might become the righteousness of God."

The result of Jesus death is that believers become the righteousness of God. Just as when the blood was placed on the lintel and sides of the door to prevent the angel of death entering the home, the blood of Christ covers those who accept Christ as Savior, surrendering authority for their lives to God. When God examines them, He sees the risen Lord in their place. Christians are totally to God, made new. As Paul states in Romans Chapter 8:1,

"...there is now no condemnation for those who are in Christ Jesus!"

Yet, God's redeemed people do not always grasp this truth. Still living in this world, people face temptations to return to soul/mind thinking rather than living in faith. Even though Christians are new creations in Christ, they have old habits in their minds and emotions which try to negate trusting God above self. Living as the redeemed of God takes practice and cleaning out old habits and thoughts. Repentance means a change of mind. Thus, when old habits return or old condemning thoughts and emotions arise, Christians are to turn to Jesus to strengthen them. For those who accepted Him as Savior and master of their lives, they become Jesus's righteousness. What a beautiful promise Jesus gives! What does this mean when old habits and thoughts arise within in a person? When individuals accepted Jesus, they gained the indwelling of the Holy Spirit. Jesus tells us in John 16: 13-14:

But when he, the Spirit of Truth (Holy Spirit) comes, he will guide you into all truth. He will not speak on His own; he will speak only what is yet to come. [14]He will bring glory to me by taking what is mine and making it known to you.

In times of slipping into old habits, thoughts, and emotions, by turning to Jesus, the Holy Spirit can give us truth. Truth is:

➢ We are no longer under the law of sin and death.

➢ There is no condemnation in us since we were bought at a precious price.

➢ We are children of God, full of righteousness.

When new creations in Christ Jesus, Christians, are assailed with old doubts leading to pits of depression, sadness, loneliness and other negative thoughts and emotions, God gives His people an example of how to handle this in one of the truths in the Bible. John the Baptist was caught in this pit right before his own death. He lost faith in his mission and lost hope. He turns to Jesus for understanding. When John was in prison, he sent his people to ask Jesus, "Are you the one who was to come, or should we expect someone else?" (Luke 7:19). Jesus replied to tell John, in Luke Chapter 7:22-23:

"22Go back and report to John what you have seen and heard: The blind receive sight, the lame walk, those who have leprosy are cured, the deaf hear, the dead are raised, and the Good news is preached to the poor. 23Blessed is the man who does not stumble on account of me."

It was to give John reassurance that Jesus reported to John's friends the prophesy in Isaiah was being fulfilled based on these results. John knew Jesus when John was in the womb of his mother. For when Mary, pregnant with Jesus, came to visit pregnant Elizabeth, the infant John leaped for joy (Luke chapter 1:40-44). When John was losing hope and overwhelmed by doubt brought on during his imprisonment, he turned to his cousin Jesus for reassurance. In his own captivity, he sought Christ. John's mission was to proclaim the coming Christ. He encouraged people to have a change of mind (repent) and be washed for forgiveness of sins. In Luke chapter 3:16 John the Baptist states,

"I baptize you with water. But one will come, the thongs of whose sandals I am not worthy to untie. He will baptize you with the Holy Spirit and with fire."

When serving the Lord, John knew his purpose, and was intent on his goal. Even when Jesus came to be baptized by John, John recognized him as the Christ for he stated in Matthew chapter 3:13–14:

"¹³Then Jesus came from Galilee to John at the Jordan to be baptized by him. ¹⁴And John tried to prevent Him, saying, "I need to be baptized by You, and are You coming to me?""

John tried to stop Jesus. On many levels and many times in his life John knew Jesus was the Christ. Yet in his moments of despair, doubt and self-criticism, John wondered if it was all worth it, or was he wrong about Jesus? Here is an example of what to do when overwhelmed with doubt, caught as captive in prison within minds and emotions, or even physically contained by the actions of others. No one is immune to these moments in their lives. Even a devout Christians has a dark night of the soul. Yet the answer is waiting for believers in the personhood of Jesus. Jesus can still bind up the hearts of the broken hearted, provide freedom for the captives (caught in self-rejection, judging ourselves less than we should be) and release from darkness (of soul and mind) the prisoners. Jesus fought the battle on Calvary, defeating not only death, but also gained all authority and power in heaven and earth. Mathew 28:18 states, *"And Jesus came and spoke to them, saying, "All authority has been given to Me in heaven and on earth."*

Satan was defeated by Jesus. His authority was stripped and given to Jesus. Since Jesus is as alive today as He was on Easter Sunday, He still has all power and authority on this earth. He can overcome anything if His people only ask.

Romans Chapter 8:32:

"He who did not spare His own Son, (Christ Jesus), but gave Him up for all of us; how will He not also, along with Him, graciously give us all things?"

Like John the Baptist, Christians need to ask Jesus for answers when full of doubt, self-blame, and rejection of self. God's people do not see clearly at these times. Believers are in a battle in their own soul. They are blinded by their own guilt and do not look to the Light of God, Jesus Christ. The only way Satan can re-gain power in this world is by each person accepting one's guilt as unredeemable and turn away from the power and authority of Christ Jesus is in this world. Thus, Satan accuses people of wrongdoing, wrong thinking filling them with doubt, uncertainty, confusion, blame and regret. Turning to Jesus clears Christian's mind. This is the definition of repentance, a changing of the mindset. As it states in Romans chapter 8:31:

"What, then, shall we say in response to these things? If God is for us who can be against us?"

Defy Satan and claim Jesus! Do not empower self-rejection, shame, and someone else's guilt. By turning over all these things to Jesus, claiming a person's right as a son or daughter of God, these things lose power. Remember what Jesus said to John, *"blessed is the man who does not stumble on account of me"* (Luke 7:23). On account of Jesus, who accomplished through His sacrifice, overcoming the grave, defeating Satan, and being handed the keys to all power and authority in Heaven and earth, we are blessed. Christians do not have to stumble, nor do they have to struggle with guilt and shame. Take Jesus into one's mind and heart as the healer He is.

One of Jesus's disciples wrote about this very struggle. Disciple John sought to reassure those who had claimed Jesus as Lord and Savior that the devil, Satan had no power over them. In 1 John chapter 3:8-9,

"8The one who does what is sinful is of the devil, because the devil has been sinning from the beginning. The reason the Son of God (Jesus) appeared was to destroy the devil's work. 9No one who is born of God will continue to sin because God's seed remains in him; he cannot go on sinning because he has been born of God."

Though the devil no longer has authority over the earth and those who claim Jesus as Lord and Savior, he still attempts to destroy people through their soul mind. Dwelling on failures, accepting other people's judgement of one's actions or lack of actions as unworthy, not enough, unloving or any other guilt-based results is allowing a crack in the protection Jesus gives His people. Flee quickly from this mindset! Each new creation in Christ has the seed of God in the form of the Holy Spirit within them. Call on His power to repent and turn to Jesus.

3

Pleasure's Lure

Pleasures have an allure, giving one satisfaction, supporting opinions of self, and creating a sense of "feels good." People seek enjoyment. They desire something that "feels good". This can be at any sensual level, whether food, drink, touch, sound, or sight. It can be relaxing, smoothing out the stress in people's lives. It can be exhilarating, challenging a person physically, mentally, or involving one's emotions like a roller coaster ride. Sometimes pleasure is achieved with success in business, competing with others. Sometimes it stretches people to do more than they think they can accomplish. This higher plateau of success is described as a "natural high". Many times, people describe the pleasure filled activity or event as something they have earned or is owed to them. The variety of what activities, challenges, events, or substances that are related to what someone claims gives pleasure is a varied as there are individuals and cultures on this world.

At first, in the early stage of pleasure seeking, a number of satisfactions result from the events, substances, or activities that provide pleasure. There is calmness that one describes as peace. There is a sense of personal satisfaction. Others have a sense of joy. Some experience an exhilarating burst of completeness of self. They "feel good" about being who they are and where they are in their lives. Over time, continued repetition of the activity at the same level fails to provide that overwhelming sense of satisfaction first experienced. More frequent events, or activities, or use sometimes seem to raise the bar of satisfaction. Eventually, over time, increasing frequency or intensity of the pleasure loses the "best" or "exceptional feeling". Sometimes people pursue it hoping that once again it will be exceptionally good. If that does not happen, people believe the lie that somehow, they are not doing it right or the source they are using is somehow inferior to what they had before. As the lack of original level of satisfaction or high continues, people become disgruntled, dissatisfied with life. Many times they blame others or situations for the lack of calmness or joy they are not receiving from their pleasure satisfier.

People have hidden from themselves a belief that they have a right to the sense of "good feeling" they receive from the pleasure activity. They begin to deceive themselves. People no longer examine all the parameters of why the amount of attention placed into an activity is producing less of the desired outcome. It is all about personal satisfaction. They like to feel good and have pleasure. During the early stages of using one's chosen form of pleasure creators, the activity gives one a sense of empowerment. When they use it after emotionally feeling down, lonely, or other negative emotions, at first, people feel better. When used as a celebration, something they earned or deserved, the beginning use has the added bonus of not only satisfying a pleasure but giving an emotional high to self. Some might justify by saying, "Hey, I deserve this and earned this pleasure." When people begin to see physical side effects from their pleasure satisfier, many times they cover them up with rationalizations. Some might claim, "it is not so bad to have this desire, at least I am not......" or "I only have this one pleasure. Surely God would not deny me my one pleasure in life?"

What started out as an activity to create personal pleasure gradually can overtake one's life. The activity becomes a beast demanding of time, money, and energy. A number of traps in personal thinking help one maintain the delusion one deserves this pleasure at all costs. The first trap is not seeing that the seeking of pleasure is self-focused. The second trap is justifying when confronted with the destructive results of excessive use of the pleasure creator. The results of justifying one's actions in one's head further separates a person from God and others. People become caught in a mentality of denial. Some might say, "not only do I deserve this pleasure, but I have also earned it and no one or nothing has the right to demand I give it up or modify when I choose to use it!" People build walls around themselves, avoiding those who care about them and ask them to be vulnerable with them. Some people then isolate, judge others, and separate themselves further from God. These individuals seek only others who are just as self-focused on the same pleasure creators. These people agree with each other's understanding and justifications. The third tier in the destructive process of excessive pleasure-seeking activities is an attitude of blaming others and events for the pleasure one seeks as not being as satisfying as it used to be. This blaming and disgruntled relationships with others increases walls of separation from caring people. The separation's effect causes one to be more judgmental. Unfortunately, those caught in this third level are only left with the pleasure creating activities that cannot meet all their needs. Bitterness grows in their hearts, fueling more separation from God.

Humanity is first spirit, though residing in a physical body. If one is honest, there is a drive in each person to unite with something greater than self. These pleasure giving activities sometimes satisfy the physical body needs. Other times it satisfies the soul through feeding pride. They are connected to a person's soul by involving the will (Within the domain of the soul). Sometimes the seeking of "feeling good" may be the beginning driving force rather than the physical pleasure. Sometimes the driving force may be a sense of intellectual superiority. The desire may lead to seeking mastery over other people's thinking. Other times it may be a drive for accolades from society for personal achievements. Whatever the drive, the soul is connected through the will to maintaining these activities. A pattern begins:

➤ A desire is satisfied

➤ Creating a sense of satisfaction invades and feeds the soul.

➤ There is a need to repeat the satisfaction.

➤ Satisfaction reinforces a backward nurturing of self from outer to inner being.

➤ The spirit is left undernourished.

➤ A vague sense of dissatisfaction forms, as the result is not united with one's spirit.

When people focus on the physical/soul level and value it more than the spiritual, they enter into spiritual warfare. There is no middle ground for a Christian. John, one of Jesus' disciples wrote about this process in I John 2:15-17,

"15Do not love the world or anything in the world. If anyone loves the world, the love of the Father is not in him. 16For everything in the world— the lust of the flesh, the lust of the eyes, and the pride of life—comes not from the Father but from the world. 17The world and its desires pass away, but whoever does the will of God lives forever."

Notice John starts describing the process as the cravings or desires. After being physically satisfied with an activity, substance, or success, one craves more. People want to repeat the sense of satisfaction again and again and again. Now the inner being, the soul, has been connected to the satisfaction. There is passion connected to the event and a person's will power seeks this physical and emotional high again, as illustrated by the lust of the eyes. One only has to look into the eyes of someone filled with desire to find this truth. This is an outward manifestation of the inner desires and longing now in the soul. Lust of the eye can also be desire for power, or prestige in society. It is an intellectual satisfaction in the mind, manifested in controlling others. This follows the same pattern of corruption within the soul. Power over others can be intoxicating to some people. John describes the final third level as pride in boasting in self-achievement and success. All three soul parts are now entangled. The will wants to keep repeating the pleasure satisfiers. The heart keeps seeking more emotional satisfaction or highs. The mind is seeking greater accolades and approval for personal success from the people of the world. The end result is becoming self-absorbed and self-orientated. The Bible labels this end result of self-absorption as hard-hearted.

This is the opposite of what Christians are called to be as followers of Christ. Those who acknowledged Jesus as Lord and Savior have died to self. They turned their wills over to Jesus. This is where the spiritual warfare for each of person happens. Though many may not be conscious of the cause of dissatisfaction, this backward seeking of joy and pleasure from the body into the soul and denying the spirit, is still real.

Jesus came to answer and help humanity in this battle. John, one of the original disciples, wrote in I John 3:8–9:

"⁸He who does what is sinful is of the devil, because the devil has been sinning from the beginning. The reason the Son of God appeared was to destroy the devil's work. ⁹No one who is of God will continue to sin because God's seed remains in him; he cannot go on sinning because he is born of God."

Remember sin is continually, willfully choosing self over God. It is rebellion from the ordained balance of creation. When people believe their right to place their wants, needs, opinions and actions above their relationship with God they willfully choose self over God. It is in disharmony with humanity's primary relationship with God. Please do not think, not sinning means giving up a person's wants, desires, and needs. God will provide for them in more abundance and in richer quality than we ask. As stated in Philippians 4:19:

And my God will meet all your needs according to the riches of his glory in Christ Jesus.

It is where one's priority lies, or what is in the heart that determines sin. Basically, continual self-focus leads to separation from God. One side of this spiritual battle, the devil and all his works, chooses to challenge God. The devil and his angels desire to create an alternative kingdom outside of the authority of Creator God. Satan chooses earth as his possession. To achieve this occupation, he needs to control humanity. Keeping humanity primarily focused on soul/physical pleasures and denying the spiritual realm allows him to control humanity. Father God sent His Son Jesus to destroy the devil and his power over humanity. Those of us who have chosen to serve Father God, honor Jesus, and listen to the Holy Spirit, are on the other side of the battle. There are no conscientious objectors in this battle. They that think they are neutral are prisoners of the devil in mind, emotions, and bodily disorders.

Remember, God knows each person in heart and mind and still loves people. Throughout history, as recorded in the Old Testament, God has been interacting with His people and knows their weaknesses. He knows His people's desires.

Through His wisdom, Jesus simply states what we need to do in order to satisfy our relationship with God and meet our desires. In Mathew 6:33, Jesus states:

But seek first the Kingdom of God and His righteousness, and all these things will be given to you.

In the three levels of remaining in harmony with God, the first level is harmony in relationship with God. Seeking God and His kingdom honors the first level of harmony. God understands this spiritual battle His people face. It is a battle when an individual's physical body and soul body are enticed to rule over one's spirit body. Through Jesus Christ's death and resurrection, people receive salvation, righteousness and Jesus' authority over Satan and this world. Under Jesus' cover of His redeeming blood, His people can be overcomers. Once individuals have that straight, God will more than abundantly provide the desires of their hearts. God promised that Jesus came that His people might have life and more abundantly than individuals now know (John 10:10).

Saying no to controlling and excessive worldly pleasures and passions is difficult. People are not called to a puritan understanding of the world where worldly pleasures are suspect and possible traps for serving the devil. Rather, when the desire and pleasures take precedence over God, His people are called to decide where their hearts lie based on how they spend their time and money. Nurturing one's relationship with God becomes a person's first desire. It is when things become obsessive, valued, and honored before one's routine of building a relationship with God, that the lure of pleasures requires reexamination. Listed below are some examples of making worldly pleasures into demigods.

➤ Planning all my free time, outside of work or school around shows on TV, sporting events, video games, social media, and giving them priority over time I spend time with God in prayer, or Bible study or church activities.

➤ Spending my money on my pleasure creator items I crave and believe I deserve, instead of meeting my financial obligations for basic living arrangements.

➤ Prioritizing time with others above regular time with God.

➤ Placing priority on time working out to improve my body over time spent with God.

➤ Never missing a Friday after work celebration. Drinking at my favorite bar or dinner at our favorite restaurant but sleeping in on Sunday and missing church.

These are a problem when one is convicted to modify excessive time with pleasure creators and finds it difficult to accomplish. One might misunderstand, letting go of excess pleasures is a process not necessarily an event. Paul in Titus 2:11-13 describes a process,

"¹¹For the grace of God has appeared that offers salvation to all people. ¹²It teaches us to say" No" to ungodliness and worldly passions, and to live self-controlled, upright and godly lives in this present age, ¹³while we wait for the blessed hope—the appearing of the glory of our great God and Savoir Jesus Christ."

In the process one trains to renounce ungodly and worldly passions. Please note again, these are the passions that chain one to self-centeredness, crippling a person's soul, so choice and will are subsumed by the sensual/mind desires. It does not mean Christians will not have enjoyment or pleasure in their lives, but rather it is to be in balance. God created humanity to have joy, fun, laughter, and physical pleasures. He wants His people to enjoy the world He gave them. The difference is that God wants His people to place it in the proper order in their hearts. He knows when this backward approach to satisfying personal desires is from the outside inward, people will end up in bitterness, separation from others and resentment. As Jesus states, he came to set the prisoners free. His death was a way to free people chained to this cycle of seeking and partially satisfying desires, crippling their souls and turning a being who is first spiritual into something depending on physical/soul satisfaction. He accomplished this and more at the cross where the innocent flesh of Jesus was crucified for anything that separates us from God. By accepting Jesus' actions, this cycle is broken, and the prisoner is set free. Then the journey of learning how to open one's eyes and heart for Jesus begins and is guided by the Holy Spirit. Jesus said on the cross, "It is finished." His sacrifice ended the need for the enticing flesh/mind driven desires that overwhelm people. Take up Jesus and enjoy rescue from what keeps a person prisoner to one's flesh/soul bodies. Jesus stated his burden is light. By joining with Him, a believer is a new creation and has freedom.

4

Emotional Entrapment

Ephesians 6:12

"For our struggle is not against flesh and blood, but against the rulers, against the authorities, against the powers of darkness in this world and against the spiritual forces of evil in the heavenly realms."

The enemy of God, the fallen angel Satan, is cunning and manipulative. He is great at delusions, intimidations, and lies. As long as he can direct a person's gaze on other people, through events and relationships, individuals will fail in trusting the provisions of God. When caught in perceived disrespect from others in any situation, individuals will fail to know they are in a spiritual battle. The thought life is the battlefield. The emotions are the buried landmines planted by the enemy as products of these situations. Caught in these events, it is easy to slip into habits of a person's past. Self-focus may rear its head. All this leads a person to focus on the earthly conditions as the source of the solution instead of trusting Father God and the living covenant with Him.

Bitterness

One of Satan's most successful tools is bitterness. Bitterness can come into one's heart when individuals do not get their own way. The moral value of an individual's way, whether noble or more selfish, really does not matter when a person is focused on getting one's own way. It is the desire to have one's own way, coupled with the belief that individuals have rights to get their own way, that interferes with one's relationship with God. This coupling places a person outside of God's ordained order for creation. It is in rebellion to God's Lordship. By demanding one's own way and believing that an individual has the right to it, people place themselves on the same plane or level as God. As Christians, this is rebellion. Our triune God is the only all knowing, all powerful and all good entity Christians recognize. By acting otherwise, individuals are the judge and jury of the events and people. This deadly coupling judges those individuals in conflict as people lacking in character. Thus, individuals give themselves permission to act as they see fit to obtain what they believe is best. Individuals are now outside God's divine will, no longer in His protection in these battles against principalities. These battles are the schemes of the enemy of God. Because people have rebelled against God's divine order, they do not achieve their goal, and bitterness enters their hearts. People who do not get what they want believe the results are unfair. It is an attitude the Bible calls a matter of the heart. In society, people get sidetracked with justifying behavior with motives. Rather than seeking further into their own heart intentions and staying in right relationship with God, people have overwhelmed God's will. Remember, God knows people by their heart! Proverbs 21:2 states,

"A person may think their own ways are right, but the LORD weighs the heart."

When a person does not get what is desired, blame is assigned to the person who stopped it. Again, whether individual motives are purer in a person's mind or society's, does not enter into the equation with God. Believing one's own motives are purer or more noble only clouds one's thinking. It is the blaming that is at issue, for it is the cause of bitterness! It starts early in individual's developing lives. Society even names the stage as the "terrible twos". It is a stage when a child begins rebelling against a parent for not receiving what the child wants! As children grow physically, this rebellion continues, as various stages of self-awareness develop. Within society there are landmark times: the beginning of teenage years in middle school, the entering of high school and becoming legally an adult. Each time children develop a more sophisticated manner of rebellion against authority than the earlier stage.

As individuals grow emotionally, they learn from their mistakes in lacking finesse in their approach to gain one's way, so they become subtler. People develop better methods of convincing themselves and others they deserve to have their own way. It is not uncommon by adulthood, to have so disillusioned themselves that they do not even know they are in rebellion for not getting their way. After all, as an adult, what are they rebelling against except unfair, unreasonable rules? These understandings are recorded in James 4:1–3,

"¹What causes fights and quarrels among you? Don't they come from your desires that battle within you? ²You desire but do not have, so you kill. You covet but you cannot get what you want, so you quarrel and fight. You do not have because you do not ask God. ³When you ask, you do not receive, because you ask with wrong motives, that you may spend what you get on your pleasures."

People are so successful in their rebellion that they do not even realize they are rebelling against God's authority. As stated in Psalm 51:4,

"Against you, you only, have I sinned and done what is evil in your sight; so you are right in your verdict and justified when you judge."

The truth is not in people when they focus on justifications, rationalizations, motives, and rights within society. The Bible states Christians are to renew their minds through capturing every thought against God (Romans 12:2 & 2 Corinthians 10:5). It is through the work of the Holy Spirit in each Christian, that one's mind is renewed. In this process Christians re-enter into a right relationship with God. God's people need to take their actions to a higher level and submit to God, for truth of one's relationship with Creator God is found in Psalm 139:1–4:

"You have searched me, LORD, and you know me. [2]You know when I sit and when I rise; you perceive my thoughts from afar. [3]You discern my going out and my lying down; you are familiar with all my ways. [4]Before a word is on my tongue you, LORD, know it completely."

Even righteous acts can be a trap if they are done outside of continual recognition of God as God, the divine creator, provider, our shepherd, our source of all goodness. Jesus states the Pharisees have already received their reward when they publicly pray (Matthew 6:5). Their prayers were to impress others, not serve God. Society recognized them as serving their own righteousness! If Christians do not fight for God's truth, they all following actions which are self-focused. Self-focus is to be wrestled from former mindsets and submitted to the will of God. Even though individuals have fooled themselves into thinking it is not about getting one's way, it is. Eventually bitterness arises.

Unforgiveness

Hebrews chapter 12:15:

"See to it that no one misses the grace of God and that no bitter root grows up to cause trouble and defile many."

Bitterness arises when individuals blame people as the source of their discomfort. They cannot separate the misunderstanding, or the lack of support they receive, from a person. It is their behaviors, not the person themselves causing them discomfort. Since it is a relationship with others, misunderstanding occurs. At least two people bear responsibility for the interactions. Jesus said to remove the plank from one's own eyes before accusing others who has a speck in their eyes (Luke 6:42). People are to search their needs to have their own way before looking to the other person. First, examine one's own motives and thoughts. Check for rationalizations or justifications in one's own behavior. Secondly, check individual emotions for pride, jealousy, and resentment. Is winning and controlling the relationship a goal in one's heart? Now it is possible to view the other person's actions more clearly. When one looks at the other person, separate actions that one deems directed against self, from the personality and relationship an individual has with the other person. All people are more than their actions. Check to see if self-satisfying desires are the goal of the person one is confronting. In these cases, individual needs of the one interacting with them may be incidental to the person committing the act. Sometimes each person wants their own way, and this is the issue, not the action. All people suffer from this problem. It leads to sins against each other. In the much-quoted statement on love in 1 Corinthians chapter thirteen, some of the definition is sometimes conveniently overlooked. As recorded in 1 Corinthians 13:4–5,

"⁴Love is patient, love is kind. It does not envy, it does not boast, it is not proud. ⁵It does not dishonor others, it is not self-seeking, it is not easily angered, it keeps no record of wrongs."

Love is not self-seeking. Pride can enter a relationship when the need to win overrules caring for the other person. Pride also arises when the person uses a defensive mechanism to cover a conviction of truth. Love is not easily angered. When a person is focused on the other person's needs over their own, anger does not arise. Anger can be a signal the person is more focused on winning an argument rather than building a relationship. Keeping a record of wrongs justifies the person's unwillingness to reconcile and return the love to another. It builds walls of separation rather than building a relationship. Carrying grudges against the person is the next downward step after bitterness.

Many times, individuals keep a record of wrongs committed against them by the other person. A record of past actions may be practiced in the mind of one person. It would include when the other person gave in to the demands of the first. Some people view giving in to the other person's desires and needs as a sign of weakness. Still others believe if they demonstrate love by doing what the first person wants then eventually, the balance will shift, and their own needs will be met. All these attitudes are "other" focused with the agenda being "getting my way". An old adage, "it takes two to have a fight", is true. Two people, unwilling to overcome their own wants, leads to conflict. The conflict exists even when one tries to ignore the other person and the events. This is known as passive aggressive control. In the mind of the one "not fighting", the person justifies oneself with such statements such as:

➢ "This is the Christian thing to do, to rise above and not fight back."

➢ "If they really love me, they will see how much I sacrifice for them by giving in."

➢ "True love means giving to the other person; if I give now, then later, they will love me back."

Over time a pattern develops. A struggle for power in the relationship happens. Many times, other people outside the original relationship are sought to hear their side and agree with "someone has done them wrong" talks. All these actions and lack of honesty of emotions, gradually destroy relationships and hardens positions. A sense of rightness in one's position of "how terrible the other person" is develops. These are all signs of unforgiveness.

People miss the point of reconciliation and forgiveness. Jesus was specific about the spiritual consequences of unforgiveness. Just after giving the disciples the Lord's Prayer he stated in Matthew 6:14–15,

"14For if you forgive men when they sin against you, your heavenly Father will also forgive you. 15But if you do not forgive men their sins, your Father will not forgive your sins."

Forgiveness like Jesus describes is total as far as the east is from the west (Psalm 103:12). It is not:

➢ I forgive the person this time, but I will not forget the wrong.

➢ I'll forgive them, if they forgive me.

➢ I am being the better person to forgive, but it's their turn next time.

➢ Love is requiring me to forgive, but I don't like it.

➢ To stay right with God, I have to forgive this person so God will give me what I want.

Nor is forgiveness making oneself into a doormat. As stated in 1Corinthians 13:5, love does not dishonor the other person. If one person in the relationship bullies the other person, constantly demands one's way, or is demeaning to the other person, this is not to be tolerated. The second person in the relationship cannot teach or love the other person into a healthy relationship while being demeaned and devalued. Jesus stated to be wise as serpents and as gentle as doves (Matthew 10:16). The serpent knows when to hide, when to attack, when to move away from trouble. It is self-protecting and deadly when attacked. The dove has nothing about it that harms others. It is self-effacing, going about its business even in tough, smog covered cities. Christians are to balance causing no harm to others with protecting themselves from those whose intent is deadly to them. Only through Christ, and the Holy Spirit's presence within Christians, can they discern what to do when. The person attacking, belittling, and demanding is functioning from multiple fears. 1 John 4:18 states,

"There is no fear in Love. But perfect love drives out fear, because fear has to do with punishment. The one who fears, is not perfect in love."

Only God is capable of perfect love. Christians follow God, love God, and try to continue in obedience. Even with the grace of Jesus Christ, His atonement and invitation into being re-created as a new person in Christ, Christians still have a human nature. Only God can love perfectly and overcome the fear that is driving one person to control another. God can help the person controlled by fears to rise above them, through reconciliation with God. Nothing is impossible for God.

Christians received the gift of grace in Jesus' death and resurrection. God's people did not deserve it or earn it. It is a choice to accept the gift. Please remember, God gave us free will and if fear-controlled people choose not to turn their whole life over to Christ, and allow God to re-create them in Christ's image, another person cannot make that happen.

Our goal as Christians is to walk in God's light, to be in fellowship with God, to serve God, and be servants where God calls us to be. 1 John 1:5b–7 states,

"⁶God is light; in Him there is no darkness at all. ⁶If we claim to have fellowship with Him yet we walk in darkness, we lie to ourselves and do not live in truth. ⁷But if we walk in light, we have fellowship with one another, and the blood of Jesus, His son, purifies us from all sin."

Christians are called to be children of God, walking in Light. To do that, God's people must start with seeking to eradicate the darkness within themselves before seeking to attack the darkness in others. Christians are to be in right relationship with others. It is only through the blood of Jesus and the power of the Holy Spirit that anyone can even begin to do this task. So is the old adage, "it takes two to fight." The question is not whether one is purer, more correct, or has the moral high ground, but rather what is one's part in the conflict? In essence, the gospel states, "I do not have the right to hang on to grudges, keep lists of the other person's failure or play it is your turn to apologize first. I did it last time". When the disciples understood what forgiveness was, they asked, "So how many times do we have to forgive our neighbor?" Jesus states: seventy times seven (Matthew18:22). In other words, it does not end until a habit is established to first see one's own part by examining one's own motives and heart, own personal mistakes, and make amends when necessary, instead of attacking and using another person's actions to destroy a relationship.

Yet, imperfect people have the tendency to lean into their own understanding. When hurt, people want to hold onto the hurt, massage it, categorize it and use it to justify their own actions against another person. This choice is unforgiveness and leads to separation from God. This is choosing darkness. Those making this choice are living in untruth. Individuals are then walking outside the protection of God and into the world. Satan wins the battle when Christians walk outside of God's path through bitterness and unforgiveness. The next choice down this dark path can lead to resentment.

Resentment

Unforgiveness is the conscious act of resting in one's thoughts and will. It is raising them as a banner to justify one's own behavior. Resentment is beyond this, layered with carefully massaged emotions, like a small snowball that is molded and shaped into a destructive weapon to be slung at the other person. It involves emotions, thoughts, justifications, rationalizations, fears and hardening of a spiritual heart. It is destructive to the person creating it. The snowball grows and hardens as these emotions, and rationalizations are reinforced daily or weekly, reminding oneself how this other person is throttling one's will and desires. To the person at whom it is directed, this destructive snowball is hurtful, vengeful and has the potential to destroy the relationship as well as grievously harming the other person. God can and will protect and heal the one this destructive snowball is aimed at if the person turns the relationship over to God. The same is true of the person who creates this resentment. Turning to God can soften the heart and bring healing and reconciliation. It is a choice.

Most often, the creator of this snowball, the one who chooses to layer unforgiveness with emotions, including fear, tries to control the situation. In order to maintain anger and bitterness, the actions of the target, the other person, is reviewed. Lists of slights, innuendos, things not said, and actions not taken as well as words said and actions taken, are reconsidered. These thoughts are appraised like a precious stone, examined from multiple points of view and with each viewing more bitterness and anger, is added increasing the size of offenses, increasing the destructive snowball. At this point, there is nothing the other person in the relationship can say or do to reach reconciliation. The builder of the snowball, or examiner of the precious lists of wrongs, chooses to harden one's heart against the other person.

By moving into the position of judging another as always lacking and not having any possibility of redemption, the creator of this resentment has crossed a spiritual boundary. Matthew Chapter 7:1-2:

"¹Do not judge, or you too will be judged. ²For in the same way you judge others, you will be judged, and with the measure you use, it will be measured to you."

From a Christian perspective, only God has the right to judge someone's actions, thoughts, and deeds. Only God knows the heart and intentions of a person. By hardening the heart, the author of the resentment is claiming equality with God and is in rebellion with God. This places the person outside of God's protection. It allows demonic principalities, who are in rebellion from God, access to thoughts and emotions of the perpetrator of resentment. As stated in Leviticus 19:16-18,

"¹⁶Do not go about spreading slander among the people. Do not do anything that endangers your neighbor's life. I am the Lord. ¹⁷Do not hate a fellow Israelite in your heart. Rebuke your neighbor frankly so you will not share in their guilt. ¹⁸Do not seek revenge or bear a grudge against anyone among your people, but love your neighbor as yourself. I am the Lord."

God warns that slander, seeking to have others agree with one's judgement of another person, is not a person's right. God adds that actions taken from this perspective are not acceptable. God alone is judge. Instead, if a person has a disagreement with another person, an individual is to bring it to the person. Again, God reminds His people to find peace by seeing others in eyes of love. Notice the standard of love God uses is as much as one loves oneself. As stated in Mark 12:29-31,

[29]The most important one," answered Jesus, "is this: 'Hear, O Israel: The Lord our God, the Lord is one. [30]Love the Lord your God with all your heart and with all your soul and with all your mind and with all your strength.' [31]The second is this: 'Love your neighbor as yourself.' There is no commandment greater than these."

It is the demanding of having one's way and controlling others for self-ambition that creates these situations. God now states to apply that driving force to hold the other person as precious as one does oneself.

The rebellion that began in seeking one's own desires now births a hardened heart. God warned His people concerning hardened hearts when they left Egypt. God does not change. His standard for human behavior is still the same. There are still consequences for rebellion against His divine order. As Paul asked in Romans, Chapter 6, "Should we go on sinning so that grace may increase?" He answers no! Romans 6:2:

"By no means! We died to sin, how can we live in it any longer?"

Choosing rebellion by hardening hearts is choosing to consciously sin against God. Peggy Joyce Ruth wrote in her book, Psalm 91 (page 36),

"Self-will and rebellion will keep us out of the secret place of protection because self-will is a wall we build between God and ourselves."

As long as God's people hang onto the wall of self-will, God cannot enter into a close relationship with them. God honors our choices and does not force himself on people. God wants each person to desire Him and honor Him out of free will. God will not go against His nature. When His people choose self-will over God's will, they cannot access God's blessings.

Anger

Hard-hearted people who choose self-will over God's will tend to bury guilt and doubt deep within their souls. Some are so successful at the burial that even denial of burying guilt no longer surfaces in their conscience. This takes active energy, reviewing the lists of grievances against the targeted person. Shutting out any information that conflicts with the hard-hearted person's perception of reality requires action. There is little peace in the mind of someone always looking to stifle conflicting information. Fear and anxiety grow in their souls. This creates a boiling kettle of anxiety, fear of being discovered, lack of joy and lack of confidence in themselves. It uses energy and wears out the one who chooses self-will and control over God's will.

As time progresses, the boiling kettle needs an outlet. This outlet is anger. Just as resentment was cold and calculating, this stage of trying to control other people, sources of information, interactions with others and between others, creates heat. It escapes as anger, blaming others and justifying their own point of view. A small fear of others finding out or deciding the targeted person is "not so bad" invades the soul of the one pushing down guilt and doubt. However, the person is not aware of this process. Fear begins to dominate every thought. "What if" scenarios, imaginations of situations not having taken place, are rehearsed before activities even occur. This fear drains the hard-hearted person's energy while fueling the heat of resentment, creating more anger and short tempers. At this point many hard-hearted people will become action oriented. This energy is used to destroy and limit those perceived as threats to them and their lifestyle.

There are struggles to make sure all others know the one harboring resentment is correct in their lists of wrongs and the actions they choose based on the list. Generally, the person holding on to resentment feels justified in putting down the other person and magnifying one's own value. People are placed on scales of comparisons, and the targeted person is always found wanting in moral value compared to the one judging. Self-righteousness as well as comparing types and kinds of sins others commit are discussed. Jesus told the story of the prodigal son (Luke 15:11-32) to illustrate many truths. One truth was that the older brother was angry his father threw a feast and slew the fattened calf for the lost brother. The older brother grew angry and refused to enter the celebration. Luke Chapter 15:29b-30 states,

"²⁹Look! All these years I've been slaving for you and never disobeyed your orders. Yet you never gave me even a young goat so I could celebrate with my friends. 30But when this son of yours who has squandered your property with prostitutes comes home, you killed the fattened calf for him!"

As the story reports, the anger of the older son, for doing what is correct and not being honored, is fueled by his resentment for his brother leaving with half the inheritance. The older brother harbored resentment all this time as he continued to obey his father. He buried his resentment while he glorified himself for being the better son. The oldest also describes his own actions as "slaving," implying he believes himself abused by the load of work he has completed. The anger boils out as the older son accuses his father of not recognizing and honoring his service. He places his brother on a scale with himself and finds him lacking. The older brother decides the younger brother's sins are more heinous and then pounces on them. He fails to examine his own heart, his possible pride, and self-righteous, smug attitudes. By focusing on his brother's faults, he fails to examine his own heart in relationship with the father. The parable is a great illustration of how hard-hearted people fool themselves by denying their own resentment, harbor unforgiveness, and hinder a healthy relationship with the father.

Jesus' example with the Pharisees and teachers of the Law highlights another action hard-hearted people commit as they lean into their own understanding and raise the level of someone else's sins above their own, as explained in John 8:3–11. A woman caught in the act of adultery is brought before Jesus as he teaches within the temple. Guaranteed of a large audience for their confrontation of Jesus, the Pharisees first state the Law from Moses, then the prescribed punishment, stoning. They then ask Jesus what does he say? In essence, the Pharisees are saying, "here is the rule, this person broke it, so do you support the rule God gave His people or does your sense of compassion that you are teaching stop you?" They dared Jesus to dispute a rule set by God. Imagine how justified and better these men believed themselves to be than this sin-filled woman! After all, they followed all the rules, they honored God and taught the people how to follow the rules. In their own eyes they believed God was pleased with them. Jesus answered in John 8:7,

"When they kept on questioning him, he straightened up and said to them, "Let any one of you who is without sin, be the first to throw a stone at her."

Jesus is reminding God's people of their first responsibility in relationship with God: Love your God, obey your God.

Before anyone can begin to be in relationship with others, they need their eyes on God. It is more important to make sure a person's first love is intact and in a healthy relationship with God. God made the second greatest commandment to love others. Loving God is the first and therefore the steppingstone into relationships with others. If one believes they have the right to judge others' inadequacy in meeting God's directive, one better check one's own actions first. In this incident, Jesus is highlighting another basic understanding found in Proverbs 4:20–23, *"[20]My son, pay attention to what I say; turn your ear to my words. [21]Do not let them out of your sight, keep them within your heart; [22]for they are life to those who find them and health to one's whole body. [23]Above all else guard your heart, for everything you do flows from it."*

Hard-hearted people have turned their backs on the living God. Instead, they respond more to a god that supports their own understanding of following rules and relying on their own strength. Their goal is to avoid their own guilt and bury their own doubts. This raises denial to such a height as to not even recognize they are in denial. A living God, who sent a

Savior to pay the ultimate price for humanity's sins, to die for them, does not allow His people to remain unmoved and self-focused. Another god is created full of rules and outward signs of approval. It is necessary for this made-up god to rank sins. Turning to the heart of the matter is too threatening for this attitude. The hard-hearted people magnify their strengths to others whose good opinion is sought. Even though the fears of discovery of their own guilt have increased, the hard-hearted people believe if others know their point of view, the opinions of others will drown out the fears bubbling up within their own souls.

Thus, anger reigns in the soul of these hard-hearted people. There is a battle constantly going on in the soul, to prove the rightness of their own opinions against the love of a sacrificial God who would send His only Son to die for all people's sins. Anxiety and lack of peace is buried deep within a heart that is no longer truthful to itself. This begins the disharmony on the second level, denying who a person is in Christ and God. The second level of harmony centers on accepting Jesus as your Savior. In John 1:12 it says,

"Yet to all who received Him, to those who believed in His name, He gave the right to become children of God; not born of natural descent, nor the human decision or a husband's will, but born of God."

Through the sacrifice of Jesus' death and resurrection, and accepting and believing this truth, a person can become a new creation in Christ. Denying this truth places people in disharmony with God, and now themselves, for the truth is not in them. As stated in 1 John 1:10,

"If we claim we have not sinned, we make him out to be a liar and his word is not in us."

Instead of living in truth, the hard-hearted person lives in a fantasy of who they are as a person. The lies and untruth focus on rules of living, completing charitable acts of kindness, proving, and earning salvation by works alone. Pride is the weft that weaves this belief system together along with levels of achievement or failure. This fantasy belief of self not only supports a person's own actions but also judges others as not good enough due to their unforgivable sins. It is the fuel that maintains anger as the pinnacle of bitterness, unforgiveness and resentment.

In Matthew chapter five, Jesus gives the beatitudes to the crowd. He tells his disciples he has come to fulfill or complete the law. When describing people's relationships with others, he switches the judgement from the person evaluating another person's actions onto the person judging. In Matthew 5:22, Jesus explains in depth the intent of the law.

"But I tell you that anyone who is angry with his brother or sister, will be subject to judgment. Again, anyone who says to a brother or sister, 'Raca,' is answerable to the court. And anyone who says, 'You fool!' will be in danger of the fire of hell."

Jesus is warning God's people that they do not have the right to judge another person's sins. He is portraying the level of anger described in the previous section. Nor do God's people have the right to beat someone up emotionally, stoning them, with their self-righteousness. Only God has this right to judge. Just as Jesus stated in the actions with the Pharisee, "if you examine your own heart first, you will see your own imperfections". Go to God first and deal with your own guilt. Pride of being a good person is a stumbling block. It places a person above Jesus on the cross, in essence stating, "I am so good I did not need Christ to die for my sins!"

James further explains in James 1:20,

"For human anger does not bring about the righteous life that God desires."

Jesus' death on the cross brings people back into right relationship with God when they accept Jesus as personal Savior and Lord. Placing sins on a scale of importance and placing rules and laws above one's relationship with God causes disharmony. This is again the first order of disharmony, not being in right relationship with God. It violates the first commandment as well as the second level of disharmony, denying who God's people are in Christ. When people accept that Jesus died for all people, for all time, for all sins, now their relationship with God is utmost in their lives. It is not a smorgasbord of choices to fit one's own self-will. Anger needs to be sacrificed along with self-will for the hard heart to be broken and realigned with God's will.

5

Hard Heartedness: Choosing Self Over God

Deuteronomy Chapter 30:19-20

"This day I call heaven and earth as witnesses against you that I have set before you life or death, blessings and curses. Now choose life, so that you and your children may live and that you may love the Lord your God, listen to His voice, and hold fast to Him. For the Lord is your life, and He will give you many years in the land he swore to your fathers Abraham, Isaac and Jacob."

In Chapter 29 of Deuteronomy, God draws a picture of what loving God with all one's heart and soul will create in one's life. Blessing and prosperity are promised to those who obey God's will and enter into a dependent relationship with Him. This relationship requires submission to God as Lord in covenant with His Creative Order. He explains the choice is each person's choice. One leads to abundant life and the other to a life of chaos and destruction. Choosing to be outside of the creative order of the universe creates chaos. This chaos destroys harmony. Disharmony eventually brings death since life is supported in harmony with God. Just reading the passage, a person of reason would claim the choice is self-evident, "Of course I choose life!" The condition is surrender of one's own will to God's will. Though the life of loving God with one's whole heart and soul seems a simple request, people overlook the opposite of love, fear, and minimize its dynamics in their lives.

At the beginning stages of our lives on earth, individuals are dependent on an outside source, who provides for all their needs. As young children, people express their wants and needs to have them met in a timely manner. As cute and adorable as babies are, it is easy to overlook the self-focused drive within them. To survive, they rely on parents to provide food, nurturing, comfort, and warmth. Together parents provide a place to be safe and secure. Unfortunately, babies have minimal ways of letting their needs be known and thus met. The best method is to cry out. So, individuals all start out focused on the ones who provide for their individual needs. This creates a dependent relationship. As the babies adjust to their world, self as a separate unit from mother becomes clear and the need to reunite through vocal self-expressions becomes more demanding. Children learn during their first five years how dependent they are on others. In addition, they learn how to express their wants and to modify them to an approved manner.

Many factors affect how this balance of meeting the child's needs and acting in an acceptable manner within one's environment develops. Some are conscious and other decisions are reactions to stressful and dangerous situations as perceived by the young child. These choices are re-examined as children age and enter new relationships with others outside of the family. The interplay between the child and the caregivers affects how children judge the safety of their world and how to obtain what they need. Their definitions of dependency and love are also affected by this interplay. Where inconsistent behavior occurs with adults who provide care, children receive mixed messages. Unpredictability in meeting needs for children breaks a child's trust in the provider. When adults are under stress, the child receives incomplete messages and supports. Fear is born in the child's soul. Lack of trust blossoms within the mind of the child's soul. The sense of security is compromised. No one starts out in life choosing fear over love. Yet small actions taken over time build up to choosing a life governed by fear. Inconsistent actions from caregivers for similar actions on the child's part creates confusion.

Environments that suddenly become unsafe without the child understanding the cause, creates more confusion. Adults who choose to blame children for unsafe situations one time, then not the next, and another time blaming the child again, cause the child to not trust the adult.

These states of confusion, suddenly unsafe environments, and inconsistent blame creates a need in the children to control their world. Sometimes the caring adult is living under pressures that create fear and anxiety in their own life. The child, not understanding the cause, but only seeing an adult who is only available at unpredictable times may, in their young minds, move into the role of protecting the adult. In both situations, fear and anxiety become real to the child. This is not to say that a caring adult cannot change the perceptions of a child, or that memories at early stages cannot be overcome with compassion, security, and love. Nor does it say these responses only happen at an early age. At any time in a person's life, unsafe environments, blame, and shame filled relationships create fear. Inconsistent actions by those who are trusted within a vulnerable relationship can create the same confusion, anxiety, and fear. As adults, people have choices about what they want to empower in their lives. Thus, God's appeal to people to choose to love Him with our heart and souls. God is consistent, does not create mixed messages or unsafe environments. God seeks people out to depend on Him for their needs and wants, knowing the unpredictable nature of their world.

As children grow in these emotionally unsafe environments of confusions, chaos, and stress, behaviors and choices become ingrained. Uncertainty, fear, anxiety, and stress, lead to the desire to control environments and others within their world. Sometimes children practice on other children how to manipulate and control others. The child recognizes these environments as chaotic. Learned survival skills are activated in the child's mind. If children have lived in similar situations in their past, then the solutions previously learned are applied again to make some sort of order out of chaos. Sometimes other children will choose to find ways out of chaos.

In these chaotic lifestyles, there is a general lack of trust of others. Too many times of being disappointed by others who should have protected them in their past builds distrust. This lack of trust prevents children from being truly vulnerable with another person, without the safeguard of controlling them. Sometimes the lack of trust is due to loving someone who was broken spiritually and inconsistent in their own ability to love. Sometimes the distrust is created by overwhelming jealousy or sibling rivalry over limited parent attention. There are more reasons one chooses not be vulnerable to someone else. The point is, this lack of trust leads to the desire to control people and environments. A belief that if the people are vulnerable, they will be hurt, ignored, or mistreated again is grounded within their souls. Thus, fear becomes a motivator stronger than love. By choosing self-protection, controlling an environment, and attempting to control the actions of others, a person becomes what the Bible describes as hard hearted. Embracing fear is denying the healing power of God's love. It is denying a relationship with God.

Now when fear has been empowered in a life, choosing love is not so easy. Barriers and control factors, lies, and illusions cloud the soul mind of a hardened heart. The light of God, Jesus Christ, is able to shine truth and remove these shadows if the person surrenders self to Jesus. John describes Jesus as full of grace and truth (John 1:14). Spiritual truth is more powerful than anything people see in the natural. If that were not true, then humanity would not have salvation. For it is through a death 2000+ years ago that people now are forgiven and become the righteousness of Christ. This is more powerful than any mind blocks or the acts they commit. The evidence of the many healings Jesus and his disciples preformed went against natural matter. The truth of Jesus is a spiritual truth. Jesus requires us to open our eyes to him. As stated in John 1:5,

"The light shines in the darkness and the darkness has not overcome it."
Jesus is the Word of God incarnate. He is the same power that spoke the universe into being, covered with flesh. Opening a hardened heart requires reading and listening to the same Word of God as given in the Bible. God gave us the clue about how to accomplish this, by faith. As stated in Habakkuk 2:4,

"See, the enemy is puffed up; his desires are not upright—but the righteous person will live by his faithfulness."

Paul explained it further in Hebrews 11:1,

"Now faith is being sure of what we hope for and certain of what we do not see."

It is a trust in something bigger than self and what is known by physical evidence and/or reasoning power. It is saying yes to the fact that spiritual truth is more powerful than anything humanity sees in the natural. It is a knowing on a level greater than that of the soul encompassing the will, thought processes, and emotions. Those who hang onto fear only trust what is in the natural world. It is a spiritual blindness that only faith can overcome.

Other people view the statement in Deuteronomy chapter 30, "holding fast to the Lord, listening (and obeying) God" as a stumbling block. The previous verses in Deuteronomy chapter 30 verses 17-18, address this type of person.

"17But if your heart turns away and you are not obedient, and if you are drawn away to bow down to other gods and worship them, 18I declare to you this day that you will certainly be destroyed." Deuteronomy 30:17-18 Unfortunately, modern man fails to understand that worshipping other gods is an action based on underlying beliefs that may not be consciously considered or re-examined.

So much of our secular world honors self and glorifies successful people who rely on their own talents and abilities. For example, great athletes, movie and TV stars, successful band members, music performers and successful entrepreneurs who created a multimillion-dollar company, are recognized in society's media as role models for society. They earn more money and their opinion on things outside of their realm of expertise is sought. Songs, by Frank Sinatra ages ago, "I Did it My Way," or "I Am Woman Hear Me Roar," by Helen Reddy, have become classic anthems for this religion of honoring achievement and personal success. It places faith in self at the highest level in their mindsets. This is worshipping the god of self-success.

Psychology has created whole branches that teach how to self-actualize one's potential and achieve all one can be through self-directed efforts. Those who follow this doctrine state clearly, "they do not need or want a God in their lives." Some others make statements condemning those who believe in a triune God as weak people not having courage to rise to their potential. In this belief system there is no toleration for failure. Those who profess this religion have an axiom stating failure is due to not trying hard enough. Interestingly those who profess this faith also give credit to luck, chance, and some unknown cosmic force. Many have a belief that what is deemed "evil" is on equal standing with what is deemed "good" as described in Chinese philosophy as yin/yang. Yet few people who operate under these beliefs re-examine them or acknowledge them as governing beliefs. Thus, many do not see them as a god that is worshipped by their actions, thoughts, and emotions.

Some of the other minor gods can be family, work, food, alcohol, exercise, video entertainment, or watching sports. The telltale signs of these becoming gods are to understand what is worshipped. Here are a few definitions:

1.   Worship is an extreme form of love — it's a type of unquestioning devotion. If you worship God, then you love God so much that you do not question him at all. www.vocabulary.com/dictionary/worship

2.   The feeling or expression of reverence and adoration for a deity: www.oxforddictionaries.com/us/definition/american_english/worship

3.   Archaic Honor given to someone in recognition of their merit. www.oxforddictionaries.com/us/definition/american_english/worship

As stated above, worship is devotion; an emotion connected with actions. It is also honoring and recognizing the importance and merit of the object of adoration in one's life. Notice the unquestioning part of the love act listed as worship. At some time, the worshippers have decided that the object of their love deserves unquestioned love and the acts that follow out of that commitment. Few adamant sports fans would think of themselves as adoring their teams, yet based on the amount of time, money and emotions spent in contact with the sports team, the definitions fit. Listen to such a person and how much time is spent discussing the team, following the team, considering changes in the team, and judging the people who manage the team.

This is not to single out watching or following a team as the only one of those listed above as making the team a god. Focusing on family to the exclusion of anything else, becoming entwined in other family member's activities, having family members as the primary support people in one's life to the exclusion of others, living vicariously through the lives of one's children, grandchildren, nieces, nephews, and designing all activities around the time spent with family can also fit the definition of worship. Instead of reviewing each of the others listed above (which is not an inclusive list of all gods) consider the following questions to reflect if there are minor gods in one's life being worshipped.

When one examines the actions associated with worship that are demonstrated in the above activities in terms of time and money devoted to the activities and the emotional ties to the activities, a different picture of gods develops. Some questions might help clarify how these become gods. Below, substitute one of the gods listed in the beginning of the paragraph for the word "god" in the questions. If these do not fit one's lifestyle, add a different focus such as use work, watching TV, or reading as a substitute for "god".

1. Do you plan your weekly calendar around activities with God eliminating anything that would interfere with time spent each week with your god?

2. Is your first priority of the week making sure you have time with your god?

3. When saving money for other activities, do you make sure you have money for your god events before budgeting for anything else?

4. Are you willing to sacrifice time with others in order to spend time with your god?

5. Do you fantasize about events with Your god? Dream of further events that will give you pleasure when you and god achieve them?

6. Do you spend time talking to others about your god experience you had last week, joining celebrations to honor your god in groups of people?

7. Do you set goals of things you will do with your god?

8. Do you memorialize time with your god with pictures, videos, or collections of time spent with God?

9. Does your home and car reflect your loyalty to your god?

10. Are you jealously guarding time you spend with your god, justifying in your mind your right to place god first in your life as something owed to you?

There are more questions one can ask to determine if something is a god. The point being that people may not worship rain or weather and make sacrifices to them, but sacrifice of major time, money and energy for these things may make them into gods. As warned in Deuteronomy, these actions, emotions, and time spent turns one's heart away from a relationship with the triune God. It does what the Bible calls hardening one's heart. It cuts off one's sensitivity to others and to the living God. It is worshipping something other than the triune God. As stated in Deuteronomy 30:17 - 18, these actions are choosing chaos and soul destruction.

God warns throughout the Bible of the results of hardening hearts against Almighty God. Yet in Romans, Paul summarizes God's attitude towards those who choose to hang onto fear, honor minor gods and close their eyes, ears, and hearts to our sovereign triune God. Romans 1:18:

"The wrath of God is being revealed from heaven against all the godlessness and wickedness of men who suppress the truth by their wickedness, since

what may be known about God is plain to them, because God has made it plain to them."

God's wrath is powerful. Obeying, submitting, and honoring God is a requirement of harmony within this world. It took God becoming man, in the form of Jesus Christ, to become a substitutional, unblemished sacrifice, and facing a horrendous death on a cross to absorb all the wrath and curses humanity brings on themselves when they ignore God's requirement of honoring and obeying God. Only through the spiritual process of accepting Jesus as Lord and Savior do people return to right relationship with God. Choosing self-centered hard heartedness and suppressing truth is costly! In John 3:36 Jesus Himself stated,

"Whoever believes in the Son has eternal life, but whoever rejects the Son will not see life, for God's wrath remains on him."

The life is not simply life after death. It includes a quality of life one obtains only when surrendering self to God's authority. When the Holy Spirit enters a person who chooses Jesus, submitting to Jesus' authority and will, the Holy Spirit instructs and brings gifts. Jesus talks of the peace which passes all understanding that the world cannot give as one of the gifts. (John14:27). The quality of life of a believer who spends time following the leanings of the Holy Spirit, who reads and meditates on God's words, and daily submits to God, not only obtains this peace, but also a joy, and emotional and physical health. There are more benefits, beginning with God seeing each believer as the Righteousness of Christ. Many other authors have written about this process of active grace in the life of a believer, so it will not be examined here.

As stated in the beginning of this chapter, each person faces a choice. Thank God that choice can be re-visited when a person has chosen hard heartedness. Jesus stated He is the door and those who choose Him will have abundant life (John 10:7-10). People can let go of these false gods they worship and the fear that controls them. It is a choice to release the desire to control others in order to be safe and loved. God is calling people to choose life.

6

Self-Hatred: Choosing Continual Punishment

How does a person start hating self? When do things go so wrong in life that a person believes they earned constant rejection? What are the keys within the belief that one's behavior has earned a person continual punishment?

1. Is it constantly being told no matter how successful one is, if one did one just one more thing they would be loved?

2. Is comparing oneself to a parent and finding no matches in ability, beauty, skills, and other attributes honored by others?

3. Is it from others continually rejecting a person and then blaming oneself for earning the rejection?

4. Are the expectations placed by others too high and does the person accept that one is never going to meet these expectations and has earned rejection?

5. Is it a belief a person needs to be perfect? Is it not being able to obtain outstanding success and constantly focusing on individual shortcomings?

6. Is it noticing a person is not valued and loved by others and blaming themselves for the other person's unwillingness to enter into vulnerable relationships?

7. Is it being a product of the abusive cycle in relationship: first accused of things one did not do and has no control over; then forced to defend all actions; then ridiculed, put down, insulted, and belittled with the other person unwilling to forgive and forget?

8. Is it the result of a parent who refuses to care for and love children?

9. Is it competition with a sibling and finding one is always losing or lacking the skills and talents necessary to win?

10. Is it valuing winning above relationships, success above love, taking instead of giving and finding loneliness as the end product?

11. Is it not fitting in with a group of people because of one's lack of talent in a given area?

12. Is it isolation from others due to lacking social skills, and not having the understanding or help of another to find the ways to fit within a group?

13. Is it believing one's skills earn a person love and when a person can no longer perform those skills, one is unlovable?

14. Is it belief that a person is only lovable when one behaves in a certain manner?

15. Is it continual rejection by multiple people for behaviors others do not tolerate and a person chooses not to stop?

16. Is it incest with family members at an age when one cannot choose or stop it?

17. Is it sexual attacks by others while caring friends and relatives blame the victim?

18. Is it defining oneself by keeping rules and laws and finding one always falls short?

There are multiple reasons and events that set into motion a process that leads to self-hatred and a belief that the person deserves to be rejected and punished by others. In U.S.A. society, where individualism, earned success, and talents are honored, this society can be a breeding ground for self-hatred unless it is tempered by a spiritual relationship with the living triune God. Community, as a cultural entity, is not valued or honored in U.S.A. society. Thus, what occurs in groups, whether it is family units or neighborhoods, is no longer a modifying influence on a people's judgement of their own value and place in society.

Peer pressure is a negative factor that pushes a person to remain silent about offenses committed against one. Peer pressure can also be so destructive that there is an advantage for an individual to attack a more timid member of the group.

Those caught in the bondage of thoughts and attitudes that one is unworthy to be loved, or deserves to be ignored, does not have a healthy way, in our society, to overcome these debilitating attitudes and mind sets. Our secular society does not have a mitigating force to provide positive intervention in this process of believing one deserves to be rejected and receive only conditional love.

What is conditional love? It is love and approval only when and if a person meets someone else's expectations and needs. Those caught in self-hatred believe this is the only kind of love they will ever receive. One of the items on the list above or a combination of the items in the list has become ingrained in the person's thinking to the point of affecting their expectations and beliefs. The person views oneself less worthy of love. An attitude of settling for whatever someone else will give them, rather than being alone develops. At some level, the person knows this is not really love but assumes this is all one deserves. If they believe the questions listed above, chances are they grew up in conditional love. Not knowing any other kind of love but conditional love and having a condemning outlook on self, results in a person accepting conditional love.

Another response to living through the situations described above is anger and self-protection. This response leads a person to choose controlling their environment and the people within it to make sure they will be safe and loved.

Someone who wants to control the environment and the people in it in order to feel safe and secure, are drawn to those who settle for conditional love. These givers of conditional love use love as a weapon to control a relationship. Many times, the person giving conditional love deems something about themselves as unlovable, thus it needs to be hidden. Sometimes the controller will enter into a love relationship with another person who gives unconditional love. Then another phenomenon happens. A part of the controller fears the love freely given by the other person might end or disappear. The conditional lover seeks to control the one giving unconditional love (healthy love). Another fear of the one giving conditional love is there is only so much love available and if it is shared with someone else, it will dry up. This fear of limited love causes the controller to limit whom the unconditional lover may spend time with and when it may happen. By controlling when love is given back, the one full of conditional love believes they will always receive love on their terms. Only fear is uncontrollable. It breeds more anxiety and fear. There are always more situations, events and unexpected consequences in life that create more anxiety in the heart of the one giving conditional love.

Conditional love is a human response that feeds on negative energy. This type of love is seeded with fear, punishment, rejection, and self-condemnation. If both people in the love relationship are giving conditional love, it is self-focused on the part of both participants. From a Christian perspective, self-focused attitudes and actions are in disharmony with the new covenant created by Christ Jesus in His death and resurrection.

When individuals fully accept Jesus as Savior and Lord, they willingly give their lives and wills over to Him. By accepting His sacrifice, His death, and His blood, Christians are redeemed and righteous in God's eyes. The old way dies, and a new relationship develops, loving God first, even before self. God first loved His people unconditionally with this sacrifice since no one earns it or deserves it. Christians only response to this type of love is to fall on one's knees, overwhelmed with gratitude and love. The disciple John described our response in I John 4:19, *"We love because he first loved us."*

This love God gives is unconditional, knows no boundaries, and never ends. For one caught in giving conditional love, this may be the first time true acceptance has been known. Everything that was hidden and considered unredeemable is now exposed. On the cross Jesus took all the hated and shame-filled parts. He loved so much He paid the full price for every thought, emotion, and self-rejection. Jesus destroyed them on the cross. God places His Holy Spirit in each Christian when they accept Him in this manner. The Holy Spirit helps everyone overcome self-will and self-focus.

God's people grow in Christ by practicing giving themselves to God. There is no room for self-centered controlling love or self-hatred. It is sacrificed on the altar to God in gratitude and praise as they accept His gift of salvation and God's righteousness.

There are three priorities in building a healthy Christian relationship with God. The first priority is harmony in relationship with God. By learning to accept unconditional love from God and then practicing returning it to God, one's focus moves away from self-centered needs. It is fulfilling the first priority. As stated earlier, Jesus told the Pharisees a summary of all the commandments. As recorded in Mark 12:29–30,

"29The most important one," answered Jesus, "is this: 'Hear, O Israel: The Lord our God, the Lord is one, 30Love the Lord your God with all your heart and with all your soul and with all your mind and with all your strength.'"

As one learns to receive this unconditional love and actively seek God, barriers are broken, and hearts rekindled. Gratitude springs up in a heart and wonder at the difference between unconditional love and controlling, conditional love. A person is overwhelmed with the unending pouring out of God's love into the surrendered life of the individual. The third responsibility is to love others as Jesus loves. Jesus did not give this to His disciples until hours before He completed

His mission on the cross. It was after they had spent time with Jesus and understood the depth and breadth of His love that they could begin to do the same. To His disciples, Jesus gives them a greater calling. There is a desire to return this love. In John 13:34–35 it says,

"³⁴A new command I give you: Love one another. As I have loved you, so you must love one another. ³⁵By this everyone will know that you are my disciples, if you love one another."

Like the disciples, Christians also need to spend time with Father God and Jesus before they can begin this task of loving others as Jesus does. The second responsibility of maintaining harmony with God is given by Jesus to his disciples while he is with them. It is recorded in Matthew 6:33,

"But seek first the kingdom of God and His righteousness, and all these things will be given to you as well."

The second priority in staying in harmony with God is knowing who Christians are in Christ Jesus. It includes accepting the healing provided at the cross for all faulty thinking, emotional baggage and unforgiveness. It is not found in self-focus. This harmony of who Christians are in Jesus is found in seeking the Kingdom of God.

Jesus Christ does have an answer to self-hatred. God sent His only son, Jesus Christ to die on the cross for all our sins, for all time, and be a sacrifice in humanity's place so God's grace and righteousness could enter people's lives. This sacrifice is even for those people who believe they are not worth the sacrifice. Condemning attitudes learned over time are also destroyed at the cross. Any thoughts, beliefs, and attitudes that separate one from the love of God have been crucified by Jesus in His death.

For some who have been conditioned to believe they do not deserve love through their own actions, know this is a lie. God loved each person from the moment He conceived individuals in their spirit form. He carefully chose parents for each person and a physical body to match the spirit He created. Maybe a person did not know unconditional love from their family. Know that is not what God intended when He created each person. Humanity lives in a fallen world where individuals make choices. Free will is an element God put into humanity at creation. Sometimes those who raise children or taught them are broken themselves and choose only to give conditional, controlling love. This is never God's intention. He honors free will. Sometimes adults let self-interest or fear rule their lives to the point they do not recognize the needs of children. Sometimes adults are unwilling to give unconditional love. Know God sees all, knows each heart and wants to comfort everyone. God loves each person he created. He sent His son, Jesus, who knew no sin, full of love, compassion, and mercy, with His eyes on each person's needs.

Jesus willingly gave up His life in a horrible, gruesome torturous death to cover all sins, wrong thinking, and actions. He created a new covenant: His innocence and willingness to substitute for all sin, for all time, for all people in exchange for every person to have a new birth and new start in Him. When one claims Jesus as personal Savior and Lord, all sins are cancelled forever in His blood and each person puts on the mantle of His righteousness. There are further blessings from the Holy Spirit who resides in Christians too. The point is, Jesus loved each person enough to die for them. Nothing one has done or thought was too much for Jesus to overcome and negate with God.

Some may think, "that is okay but what if the person has been trying to be faithful to God, follow God's rules and be a good person, but they judge themselves as a failure? How can God take them back now?" John the Baptist stated to all who came to be baptized, "Repent, for the Kingdom of God is at hand" (Matthew 3:2). Repent means to change one's mind, to look at life differently. When a person tries to be good, follow rules, and be pleasing to God, understand one has placed oneself under the old covenant. Following rules is part of the covenant God created through Moses. The Israelites asked to be judged by their behavior and God gave the people rules. The law was meant to teach how far people are from succeeding without God's help. Paul, who studied and knew

Jewish law well states in Romans 5:20a, *"The law was added so that trespass might increase."*

It wears down one's soul and kills joy. When Jesus walked the earth the first time, He was teaching people to recognize the old and prepare for the new covenant. He stated in Matthew 11:28-30,

"²⁸Come to me, all you who are weary and burdened, and I will give your rest. ²⁹Take my yoke upon you and learn from me, for I am gentle and humble of heart, and you will find rest for your souls. ³⁰For my yoke is easy, and my burden is light."

Jesus wanted those who were worn out from trying, to turn from the old covenant and allow Jesus to come along side of them. Jesus does more than share the burden; he bears all an individual's burdens and removes the weight and pain of them from each person's shoulders. Being yoked to Jesus means allowing Jesus to pay one's price for one's failure, guilt, and regret. His death and resurrection paid the full price and gave each believer His righteousness.

In this new start, connected to Jesus, Christians no longer give energy to other people's opinion of Christians or lack of support for each person. Christians receive these blessings through unconditional love from Jesus. The change of mind or repentance in this situation is to stop trying to earn God's approval by being good, or doing right, but rather walk with Jesus. Christians are to turn over every worry and care to

Him. They are to trust God to solve issues in their lives. Instead of focusing on the stress creating problems or strategize the best solutions, look to Jesus. Allow Jesus to create the solutions. Being yoked to Jesus means Christians turn their will over to Him to lead and guide them together.

Know if an individual has accepted Jesus as Savoir, at some time in one's life, that person carries the Holy Spirit within them. Even when an individual deems oneself a failure or believes God deserted the person, the Holy Spirit was still present. He heard that person's thoughts, saw one's actions, and loved the person when that person could not love oneself. He is still there. Just turn to Him. The Holy Spirit is counselor and advocate.

Jesus stated in John 16:13-14,

"[13]But when He, the Spirit of Truth (Holy Spirit) comes He will guide you in all truth. He will not speak on His own; He will only speak what He hears, and He will tell you what is to come. [14]He will bring Glory to me by taking from what is mine and making it known to you."

So, even if a Christian does not know what to say or how to repent (change one's mind), there is help available. Just start talking to Almighty God and the Holy Spirit will fill in the blanks in one's heart and mind. Start anew. God has never turned His back on His people, and He promised never to leave a person who turns one's life over to Him.

SECTION 2

GROWING CLOSER TO GOD

7

Living in the Light of Christ Jesus

Repentance

J ohn the Baptist, Jesus's cousin, preached in the desert as he
baptized people with water in the Jordan river. As recorded
in Matthew 3:2, *"Repent for the Kingdom of heaven is near."*
How did the Jewish mind understand this saying of John's?
Through their tradition and teaching of the written Word of
God "repent" or the Hebrew word, "naham," meant "change
of heart or disposition, a change of mind, a change of purpose,
or an emphasis upon the change of one's conduct". (Vine's
Complete Expository Dictionary 1996, page 201 Old

Testament section). The word was used to describe God's repentance concerning man's actions. Whenever God chose to change His mind or His heart toward people, "naham" is used. Those seeking out John for baptism, or to observe what John was doing, would understand John was calling them to change their minds and hearts in their understanding of their behaviors and attitudes. Our modern language might combine this sense of change of mind and heart, interpreting it to mean change our attitude and thinking, or focus in another direction. In other words, to stop focusing on one's attitude toward an event or person in a self-centered manner and focus and see the event or person differently. Sometimes people describe this as putting on different glasses to see things differently. Other times it is said to turn around one's thinking (focus). Another person might state that people are looking at things backwards. All these statements are trying to capture what John meant by saying "repent." For the purpose of this book, repent will mean "change one's focus."

In other words, change one's focus from a personal understanding and focus on God and His ways. Let go of constantly seeking satisfaction and provision for life as the world encourages. Simply let go of one's own way of thinking and trusting. Trusting and depending on one's own strength builds stress. The Creator of all order, who maintains the balance of creation, will provide for His people. As stated in Matthew 6:25–27,

"²⁵Therefore, I tell you, do not worry about your life, what you will eat or drink; or about your body, what you will wear. Is not life more than food, and the body more than clothes? ²⁶Look at the birds of the air; they do not sow or reap or store away in barns, and yet your heavenly Father feeds them. Are you not much more valuable than they? ²⁷Can any one of you by worrying add a single hour to your life?"

Christians who have confessed Jesus Christ as Savior and Lord, are under a blood covenant. The Lord Jesus Christ has promised them abundant life (John 10:10). Those John the Baptist called knew covenant with God meant Father God would give protection and provision in abundance, in exchange for surrendered lives to God as King of their nation. Obedience, trust, and faith are the coinage of participation in this covenant. Yet their focus had slipped to the world and its lack instead of trusting God and His promised provision. This is rebellion and separation from the provisions of covenant. John was calling them to turn from their focus on self and return to focus on God.

From the Jewish understanding, "the Kingdom of God" refers to a promise God made to Moses when Moses was called to lead God's people, Israel, out of bondage in Egypt. Exodus 19:5-6 states,

"⁵Now if you obey me fully and keep my covenant, then out of all nations you will be my treasured possession. Although the whole earth is Mine, ⁶you will be for me a kingdom of priests and a holy nation.' These are the words which you shall speak to the Israelites."

The Kingdom of God would be the Holy Nation God would create with the people He had chosen. This is covenant with God. God would extend His provision and protection and they would submit their wills and hearts to God. Their government would reflect the rules of the Kingdom of Heaven on earth. Father God would be recognized as their Ruler and Lord. Throughout their history, the people of God were waiting for signs and wonders to indicate now was the time for the promise of God to be fulfilled. It was a compact that if the people obeyed completely, relying on God, then God would make them a Holy Nation, a separate kingdom.

John's statement was good news for those who believed him and were baptized with water in the Jordan River. Notice John did not say "The Kingdom of God was here," but rather, "near". He also clarified this understanding by quoting Isaiah chapter 40 verse 3. A hope, an expectation was born in the hearts of those who were baptized with water. Yet John made it clear that someone else would follow him whose sandals John was unworthy to tie, who would baptize with the Holy Spirit. (Mathew 3:11-12; Mark 1:7-8). Even though further events were to happen to bring about the baptism by fire, one can learn something from the preparation John completed with the people of God.

The first clue about how to live differently, after accepting Christ and turning one's will over to Jesus, is to change one's focus. As demonstrated above, it means a mind-thought-emotion change as well as an attitude change. Instead of viewing life events and people as positive or negative towards oneself, each person is to focus on Jesus. One may think that what the person did is unforgivable, but listen to what Jesus states in Luke 6:27,

"But to you who are listening I say: Love your enemies, do good to those who hate you and bless those who curse you, pray for those who mistreat you."

Of course, this is impossible without the help of the Holy Spirit who now dwells within each Christian! Many times, the first half of the definition of Love, as given in I Corinthians chapter 13:1-7 is quoted. Examining the second half of the scriptures gives understanding of what Jesus is telling believers to do.

I Corinthians 13:4-6:

"⁴Love is patient, love is kind. It does not envy, it does not boast, it is not proud. ⁵It does not dishonor others, it is not self-seeking, it is not easily angered, it keeps no record of wrongs. ⁶Love does not delight in evil but rejoices with the truth."

Notice self-seeking is listed as what love is not. Keeping records or reviewing wrongs committed against one and holding onto anger are ways for reinforcing the self-focus. The proud boasting and rudeness are outgrowths of feeding self. Jesus is telling God's people to let go of themselves by not committing these actions: hanging onto anger, keeping a list of wrongs, and being rude. Before anyone can change behaviors, they have to stop doing one thing before they can learn to do something else. The first part of "love your enemies" is to stop the unloving actions.

Here is the secret. Do not focus on the stopping, but rather, letting go. When a person thinks about not doing something, one is still focused on it. Christians throw themselves back into the legalistic approach to God by focusing on the wrong. This thinking gives the soul mind control and denies the power within the spirit to overcome. It can increase self-blame. Self-blame is still a form of self-focus. This brings Christians back to the old covenant. It is a trap to catch one's mind and thus does not allow a person to focus differently. When the thoughts of what someone has done reappears in one's mind, think of letting go and giving them to God. Some successful tricks include:

➤ Turning the thought into a balloon that releases into heaven.

➤ Using a cartoon mallet with Jesus' name on it as you smash the thought.

> Flicking it off your shoulder saying, "By the power of Jesus, thought disappear!"

> Putting the thoughts in a box and blowing it up.

These are not the only ways of giving these thoughts up to God. Using one's own imagination along with humor and power, to create something meaningful for each person, puts the old in perspective. Remember, Christians have power in the name of Jesus to destroy footholds from the devil. Laughter and Joy are tools God gives Christians to place negative ideas in their proper place.

Remember to first stop the thoughts before moving onto what to do instead. Too many people deny the thoughts and bury them into their souls or physical bodies. This causes disharmony with God. Pretending someone is not hurting a person makes one a martyr in one's own mind. This is still a form of self- focus. God is not telling His people to put up with someone hurting them, whether physically, emotionally, or maliciously, whether in work situations or with mutual friends. Unfortunately, the idea of "turning the other cheek" has been associated with a false thought of who Jesus is. Jesus never called people to be doormats and tolerate injustice and bullying. This false notion implies abuse is okay and the person receiving it is better than the one dishing it out. It also portrays Jesus as a weak, mild person who only espoused love at all costs and continual forgiveness no matter the situation. This portrait is a fantasy with no support when the total picture of Jesus in the Bible is examined. After all, Jesus turned over the tables of the money changers in the temple and caused havoc there. Jesus also provoked the leaders of the synagogue with attacks on their integrity in public. There are many more examples in the Bible. Jesus was never this meek person who allowed abuse to continue no matter what the form. Be careful of burying the thoughts rather than destroying them when they return to one's mind.

One of the toughest things to do in our society is not to carry a list of wrongs done to person from another person. Our society, through our media, encourages a "get even" or revenge mentality. Whether it is a downtrodden hero in a movie who finally overcomes a bully or an underdog who becomes wise in the ways of the enemy and outsmarts the perpetrator, our society enjoys watching the "loser" outwitting the person with more going for them. It teaches people to wait until the right moment and then get even and more. If Christians can keep the fantasy of the media industry separate from their dreams and longing, watching these types of shows can be entertaining. Unfortunately, few young developing minds are able to do this, and in them the belief that they will destroy these bullies is incorporated in their psyche. As stated earlier, for the Christian, this approach negates the turning over of a person's will to God. It allows a person to become self-focused again.

The clue for what to do instead of these self-focused actions is again in the quote from Jesus, "Pray for those who mistreat you" (Luke 6:28). The Holy Spirit inside of Christians helps them create the prayers and helps them form what to pray. When Christians sincerely desire a positive life for those who are persecuting them, the focus changes from revenge to understanding. One outcome of the prayer may be that the people attacking may not change their behaviors. Included within this outcome may be that the one who changes is the praying Christian. Over time, the Holy Spirit leads each person to better understanding of the other people.

In interactions, Christians are no longer defensive and radiating anger and fear. They reflect Jesus' light and peace into the person attacking them. No longer are praying Christians cowering in fear, thus empowering their attackers. The attacker sees Jesus within the one praying. This gives the attacker an opportunity to consider changing the manner in which they interact with a Christian. There is no guarantee the attacker will change. Free will still operates within the situation. Without prayer no opportunity for the Light of God to enter is available. Other times the results of our prayers are that the attacker changes or others become involved who aid in a change.

So how do Christians protect themselves in the presence of their enemies? Does not God state in Psalm 23:5: "You will prepare a table before me in the presence of my enemies."?

Christians pray for God's protection from those who persecute them. God has promised protection for those who believe and trust in Jesus. Yes, God protects those who turn to Him. In Proverbs 30:5 it states,

"Every word of God is flawless, he is a shield to those who take refuge in Him."

God keeps His promises to His people. When Christians turn their wills over to Him, honor Him with trust, God does not fail. While one prays for one's enemies, God is shielding each person from the destruction they would create around the praying Christian. Christians are the righteousness of Christ (II Corinthians 5:21). Christians who claim the covenant of Jesus Christ's sacrifice, death, and resurrection, can count on Almighty God. As stated in Romans Chapter 8:37,

"No, in all these things, we are more than conquerors through Him who loved us."

Trust in God's protection. Run to His refuge. Christians can count on God keeping His word. Romans 8:28 tells one of God's promises,

"And we know that in all things God works for the good of those who love Him, who have been called according to His purpose."

Faith is believing in the promises of God, trusting something outside of ourselves that Christians deem more secure, more dependable, more trustworthy, more consistent, and eternally true. Repentance is turning a person's focus off self and onto God. The action that follows is trusting God's solutions by following God's bidding, rather than one's own. It may seem unnatural and strange by world standards. It is. Looking at it from a spiritual understanding based on the word of God, is called a faith walk.

Confession

Galatians 2:20:

"I have been crucified with Christ and I no longer live, but Christ lives in me. The life I now live in the body, I live by faith in the Son of God, who loved me and gave himself for me."

Christians have verbally declared Jesus Christ as their Lord. They believe Jesus Christ is the Son of God and Son of Man, who died for people's transgressions or rebellion against God's ordained order for His creation. Christians know in their hearts and confess with their mouths that Jesus Christ rose from the dead and lives. They have chosen to leave their former ways of living and turned their lives over to Lord God. It is important to be specific with the Lord about transgressions. It is also important for Christians to confess the choices they made that caused the separation from Holy God. As it is written in 1 John 1:9,

"If we confess our sins, he is faithful and just and will forgive us our sins and purify us from all unrighteousness."

If Christians honestly believe Jesus died for their transgressions, they own the transgressions in the presence of Almighty God. Verbally claiming the actions and thoughts that are in rebellion to God's order allows one to own their part in creating the separation. Picturing the crucifixion and seeing one's personal transgressions holding Jesus there while asking forgiveness is another way of owning the transgressions. This is what it means to be crucified with Christ. As God's people list and admit what they have chosen to do, think, and believe that was against God, the list loses power within their souls. It is broken when the transgressors picture the list as the cause of the bloodletting on the cross. The blood covers the transgression as payment for the offense against Holy God. Listing these things breaks the power of shame, guilt, blame and regret. It is not just the act or thought that caused separation, but also these emotions that tag along. Many of the negative emotions that were mentioned earlier, after the original actions, anger, self-righteous indignation, blame, self-pity, and revenge are just a few of the tag-alongs entering a soul after the acts or thoughts that are in rebellion to God's Holy order in His creation.

Confession is an active interaction between Almighty God and each person. As stated in Psalm 103:1-5,

"Praise the LORD, my soul; all my inmost being, praise his holy name. ²Praise the LORD, my soul, and forget not all his benefits—³who forgives all your sins and heals all your diseases, ⁴who redeems your life from the pit and crowns you with love and compassion, ⁵who satisfies your desires with good things so that your youth is renewed like the eagle's."

Our Lord God is not giving a generic forgiveness. To accept the benefits, believers need to admit the need. Christians are to be in a living relationship with Creator God. As mentioned before, God's people are yoked to His will and dependent on Him for personal provision and protection. God already knows His people by their hearts. As stated in Jeremiah 17:10, *"I the LORD search the heart and examine the mind, to reward each person according to their conduct, according to what their deeds deserve."*

It is for God's people's benefit they name and confess these transgressions and the emotional baggage overtaking their souls. God already knows the transgression and damage it has done to the soul of each person. Part of appreciating the magnitude of the sacrifice of Jesus on the cross, is seeing one's own transgressions there. Gratitude and love springs froth from the well of one's soul-heart as a result of visualizing the transfer of one's transgressions onto the cross. As Psalm 103 states, Christians are redeemed from a pit they dug. When people harbor some transgressions in their souls and do not confess all of them, these tag-along emotions fester and build pain buddies. People hide them from their minds and deny their power. Pretending they are not real does not reduce the destructive power within them. They are still destructive and can cause major blockages in a relationship with God. God knows this and encourages His people to confess them and see them on the cross. One of the functions of the Holy Spirit is to reveal truth. As an individual's relationship with God grows, the Holy Spirit may convict a person of these hidden and buried emotions and thoughts. It is a signal from God to confess and clean up the mess in the soul.

Later in Psalm 103, the nature of God and His purposes are explained. In Psalm 103:8-10 it states,

"⁸The LORD is compassionate and gracious, slow to anger, abounding in love. ⁹He will not always accuse, nor will he harbor his anger forever; ¹⁰he does not treat us as our sins deserve or repay us according to our iniquities."

Though our God knows each heart, and each secret transgression, He is still slow to anger. His love outweighs His disappointment in the actions that caused separation from His Holy ordained pattern for His creation. He is not surprised with His people's choices. He patiently waits for them to search for Him. Remember, the second responsibility in relationship with God is to search for the Kingdom of God and His righteousness. As He waits, He also loves people. It is an individual's job to accept the grace gift of salvation in its full measure. This includes being crucified with Christ. The old ways are to be specifically denounced. God knows turning one's will and life over to Him will be a big step for many individuals. He knows what transgression baggage each person brings when someone yokes with Jesus. Now Lord God leads individuals to confess and drop those burdens at the cross to embrace His full healing.

The promises of entering into confession, and nailing one's transgressions onto the cross, are explained in the next part of the Psalm. As stated in Psalm 103:11–12,

"[11] For as high as the heavens are above the earth, so great is his love for those who fear him; [12] as far as the east is from the west, so far has he removed our transgressions from us."

When Christians truly make God the Lord of their life, yoking with Jesus and turning away from their former lives, they develop the Fear of the Lord. Fear of the Lord is awe and wonder for all God is. In other words, the Creator of all, chooses to have a personal relationship with broken people. God sees all the spots and wrinkles in individuals and gives them the death of His beloved Son to cover their unholy, unclean choices and lifestyle. Wow, what an unfair exchange! Now this God who knows every thought and heart's desires, expects surrender of will and decisions to an all-knowing and all-powerful God. Yikes! There is no hiding in this relationship! He promises a love that is greater than the heights of heaven. An unconditional love, beyond anything individuals have known is being offered. God demonstrated this love by sacrificing His beloved Son for imperfect people. To top that off, God says these confessed transgressions are removed from one's mind and soul and God's knowledge. God will not mention or remember them again. This is the benefit of true confession.

Reconciliation

After confession, Christians enter into reconciliation. In God's eyes, what was broken in their souls has been renounced and expelled. Almighty God has separated His people from the confessed transgressions as far as the east is from the west. It has no more substance in eternity. The next step is to embrace and love God. As stated in Romans 5:10–11,

"[10]For if, while we were God's enemies, we were reconciled to him through the death of his Son, how much more, having been reconciled, shall we be saved through his life! [11]Not only is this so, but we also boast in God through our Lord Jesus Christ, through whom we have now received reconciliation."

Restored to right relationship with God, as if a person had never been separated from God, is reconciliation. Christians can fully live in close relationship with God. They can embrace and enjoy a new life, free from guilt, blame and shame. Their life is dependent on Jesus Christ. Just like a person that has been continually attacked and beaten by a bully, Christians now have a defender greater than the bully. They can easily say to the world, "Have you met my best friend Jesus? He is the champion of every fight He has ever entered. He never loses and always goes before me." Jesus is Christians' defender and friend.

Part of reconciliation is total restoration of what was damaged. Where transgressions ruled in one's soul, there is now a hole. God loves His people so much He wants to fill this hole with Himself. During the last hours of Jesus' time with His disciples, He shared a special discourse with them. In this talk, Jesus asked Father God for special benefits for those who believed in Jesus as the Son of God and the Son of Man. As recorded in John 17:20–21,

"[20] My prayer is not for them alone. I pray also for those who will believe in me through their message, [21] that all of them may be one, Father, just as you are in me and I am in you. May they also be in us so that the world may believe that you have sent me."

Not only is Jesus one's best defender, but He also lives in Christians. As stated above, when they are crucified with Christ, they die to the old ways and they live in Jesus and He in them. Those holes are filled with Jesus. Christians access this blessing by acknowledging God with thanksgiving and praise.

Being a believer in Christ Jesus is actively participating in a daily relationship with God. It is a love relationship filled with the Fear of the Lord. As in any love relationship, it requires daily nurturing. Daily Bible reading feeds the souls of believers. They listen for directions as they ask the Holy Spirit to interpret this reading. Part of love is giving to the beloved. God's people accomplish this in thanksgiving and praise. Apostle Paul understood this asking for directions through prayer. One of his prayers speaks to the essence of the relationship God is seeking with each one. Remember, the second responsibility of our relationship with God is to seek God and His kingdom first. As recorded in Ephesians 3:16–19,

"[16]I pray that out of his glorious riches he may strengthen you with power through his Spirit in your inner being, [17]so that Christ may dwell in your hearts through faith. And I pray that you, being rooted and established in love, [18]may have power, together with all the Lord's holy people, to grasp how wide and long and high and deep is the love of Christ, [19]and to know this love that surpasses knowledge—that you may be filled to the measure of all the fullness of God."

God's love for humanity frees His people from the bondages of transgressions against His Holy order of creation. As Christians respond in gratitude and praise, they return this love to Creator God. This increases the union between Christians and Creator God. They are filled with love for God and His love for them. This bond of love overcomes soul mind dominance from the past. Paul states the love of God surpasses knowledge! Christians express that love in worship and praise. It becomes an urgency within each one to release that love back to God.

Walking in faith

Romans 12:2

"Do not conform any longer to the pattern of this world, but be transformed by the renewing of your mind. Then you will be able to test and approve what God's will is--his good, pleasing and perfect will."

Walking in faith is trusting God's Word and the actions recommended in the Bible to deal with life. When a person's focus remains on God, instead of thinking about solving problems on one's own abilities, a person's mind is changed. Neurocognitive research has confirmed what the Bible states: that one's thinking is recorded in the brain and this combination reflects one's state of mind. The brain is not the source of thoughts, but the thoughts form the brain. Humanity has the power of creating healthy, life giving brain waves that encourage the body to grow healthy or create destructive patterns that hinder the body. (Leaf, Carolyn 2009. Who switched off My Brain? *Thomas Nelson Publishers*) Choosing God's way over one's own way is that powerful and important. Those who walk in faith more than likely have experienced the defeat of trying to accomplish life on their own terms. These attempts may include living under stress, and in disappointing relationships. Before choosing to turn their lives over to Jesus Christ they may have wondered what went wrong in their choices to end up in their predicaments. They consciously admit their way may not have been the best and are willing to surrender to God. Through this surrender, help comes in the form of the Holy Spirit indwelling them. Paul describes how the Holy Spirit that is indwelling the redeemed man helps a person. I Corinthians 2:10b–13:

"¹⁰The Spirit searches all things, even the deep things of God. ¹¹For who among men knows the thoughts of a man except the man's spirit within him? In the same way no one knows the thoughts of God except the Spirit of God. ¹²What we have received is not the spirit of the world, but the Spirit who is from God, so that we may understand what God has freely given us. ¹³This is what we speak, not in words taught by human wisdom but by words taught by the Spirit, expressing spiritual realities with spirit-taught words."

Trusting God and listening to the prompting of the Holy Spirit takes time and practice. Christians' goals are to accomplish what Paul stated in II Corinthians 10:5,

"We demolish arguments and every pretension that sets itself against the knowledge of God, and we take every thought captive to make obedient to Christ."

God's people begin with baby steps. The first step is to think differently. God states in His word that Christians are to spend their thoughts and time doing the following: Philippians 4:4–8:

"⁴Rejoice in the Lord always. I will say it again: Rejoice! ⁵Let your gentleness be evident to all. The Lord is near. ⁶Do not be anxious about anything, but in every situation, by prayer and petition, with thanksgiving, present your requests to God. ⁷And the peace of God, which transcends all understanding, will guard your hearts and your minds in Christ Jesus. ⁸Finally, brothers and sisters, whatever is true, whatever is noble, whatever is right, whatever is pure, whatever is lovely, whatever is admirable--if anything is excellent or praiseworthy--think about these things."

Start each day by declaring who is Lord of one's thoughts, life, and will. Following these declarations with rejoicing in praise to the Lord increases one's acknowledgement of submission to God. There are many praise songs available in a variety of music venues to use. If one prefers reading, there are many praise statements easily found in the book of Psalms. There are written prayers that give glory to God as well. Remember, this advice is not the world's wisdom, but God's. During the day, as life brings stresses, turn to quotes or music that again remind a person of God's glory and give Him praise. Instead of increasing stress, natural endorphins within one's body will respond to the joy. Trust the Holy Spirit to give advice about what to do in situations. Ask God for this help in the midst of stress-creating events. This is what it means to not being anxious about anything. Arrow prayers are described as calls for help in tough situations when emotions are running rampant, or one is tempted to lean into old ways of solving problems. An arrow prayer could be a simple statement such as, "God help me now. I don't know what to do". One could also say, "But you have said, you are always with me, and you will not leave me. Show me what to do and give me your peace which passes understanding. Not as the world gives, but as you promised in Jesus's name." Prayers and petitions like these arrow prayers are heard by God.

Giving thanks and credit to God for answering individual prayers and providing for one's needs is essential in letting go of doing things the old way and trusting God's way. Sometimes this process is called an attitude of gratitude. Every day acknowledge at least five things one can be thankful for that God accomplished. Start with the easy ones like great weather, or a good night's sleep, or money to buy groceries, or a place to live. The temptation is to claim it is one's hard work at a job that provides the money for these things. The reality is that God has created all things and is in control of not only the weather but the movement of the earth, stars, sun, and time. He gives humanity the ability to breathe, the physical strength to work, and the opportunity to have a job. It is in this new understanding of God's will and not one's own will be done, that power is released. Recognizing His power in a person's life and blessing God is paramount to staying in His will. Thanksgiving for all that a person has, including opportunities, is practicing leaning into God's will. As things happen during the day, look for God sightings. These are times in the day that events ran smoothly, stress was less, and joy filled your life. Thank God for these times, too. He is the author of these events. As stated in James 1:17,

"Every good and perfect gift is from above, coming down from the Father of the heavenly lights, who does not change like shifting shadows."

As a person practices giving thanks and looking for God's favor in one's life, it will become easier to find more things that create a sense of gratitude. In one's thought life, now spend more time talking with God, looking for the direction of the Holy Spirit. It is waiting for the sense of rightness and peace that accompanies the Holy Spirit's leanings. The more time spent in these activities, anxious feelings and thoughts will lessen. Thus, the next step in this process occurs; The peace of God surrounds a Christian's heart and mind.

As stated earlier, this is a process, one baby step at a time. No one gets it right the first few times. Thank God for His forgiveness! Simply talk with God and admit times of failure. These may be times of falling back into taking charge of situations, or credit for success, or old thinking patterns to relieve stress. A sincere request for forgiveness and owning one's part, heals the relationship with God. Remember, God does not desert His people. The story of the prodigal son as described in Luke chapter 15 verses11-32 demonstrates God's love as He waits for the prodigal to return. He forgives and celebrates at the son simply turning and walking back to him. God does not even allow His people to debase themselves but restores each as heirs. Nothing can separate Christians from the love of God, even one's own failure. So, as one moves through this practice of thinking differently, acting differently, and transforming one's mind, just turn mistakes and backsliding over to God. This is applying the tools of confession and reconciliation to one's daily life. The Lord knows each person's heart and knows His people will not "get it right" all the time. Read what God states about His people's failures and weakness. II Corinthians: 12:9b:

"My grace is sufficient for you, for my power is made perfect in weakness."

This is such a loving, forgiving God! Even in personal weakness, when a person turns to Him, God's power, through the sacrifice of Christ on the cross, and the resurrection of Christ, covers us. It is greater when we are weak!

As each person matures in this process, then the end of the verse in Ephesians can be practiced. Think on what is pure and admirable. There is always the opportunity to grow in Christ, demonstrating one's love for God. Further steps in practicing the purpose of making every thought captive in obedience to Christ involves other activities. These are added after practicing the steps mentioned above. Romans 12:9-13:

⁹Love must be sincere. Hate what is evil; cling to what is good. ¹⁰Be devoted to one another in love. Honor one another above yourselves. ¹¹Never be lacking in zeal, but keep your spiritual fervor serving the Lord. ¹²Be joyful in hope, patient in affliction, faithful in prayer. ¹³Share with the Lord's people who are in need. Practice hospitality."

Growing in Christ is a lifetime adventure. God is sufficient to provide for all His people's needs as they move into a dynamic, loving relationship. The things listed here are multiplied within each person as they practice the beginning of the walk outlined above. Christians find joy in their hope of God's presence, in His record of what one experiences through His involvement in believers' lives. With a new mindset, Christians are now noticing and giving thanks for God's solutions to life situations. When under duress created by others, Christians have now learned how to pray for and support those attacking them and learn patience in this process. Being faithful in prayer as a continual dialog with the Holy Spirit, asking for help in all situations, and giving thanks and gratitude to God, God's people develop their faith. Begin now, walking in faith, trusting God to provide all needs.

8

Speaking Truth: The Word of God

A wonderful mystery and truth about the Kingdom of God is revealed in studying His Word. In the first chapter of the Bible, Genesis, God states how valuable His Word is. Into the void that became our earth, God spoke creation. Genesis 1:3 states, *"God said Let there be light, and there was Light."* In all verses describing a new item being created, the verse starts with "God said" (verses 6, 9, 14, 20, 24, 26, & 29). Thus, all existence came from God's Word. God's speech is valuable, full of creative powers. Later in John 1:1-3 it says,

"In the beginning was the Word, and the Word was with God and the word was God. ²He was with God in the beginning. ³Through him all things were made; and without him nothing was made that has been made."

Logos, or Word, is one of the descriptions of Jesus Christ. Strong's concordance describes it to mean Jesus, the member of the Godhead, expressing the thoughts of Father God through the Holy Spirit. Jewish understanding points back to the Old Testament where the Logos or "Word" of God is associated with the personification of God's revelation. Greek readers would understand this to mean not only what is spoken out loud but also thoughts within the mind. In these opening statements, John is pointing readers to a mystery that the living being Jesus Christ was both at the beginning of creation and participating in creation. All things were made through him as the Word.

John announces this very nature is present in the body of Jesus. He also states that the creative power of God is embodied in Jesus. In John 1:14 he writes,

"The word became flesh and made His dwelling among us. We have seen his glory, the glory of the one and only Son, who came from the Father, full of grace and truth."

Again, the connection between created life and the Word of God is drawn. The power of God's Word is demonstrated in the person of Jesus. That creative and restorative power became active when Jesus turned His will over to the Father for this Word to become flesh. The plan before the foundation of the earth was for Jesus to be sacrificed and pay the penalty for all humanity's willful separation from God and the acts those choices created. As stated in 1 Peter 1:18 – 20:

For you know that it was not with perishable things such as silver or gold that you were redeemed from the empty way of life handed down to you from your ancestors, 19 but with the precious blood of Christ, a lamb without blemish or defect. 20 He was chosen before the creation of the world, but was revealed in these last times for your sake.

It is through God's loving grace that humanity is redeemed in this manner.

Jesus demonstrated this truth in His recorded confrontation with Satan, in Matthew 4:4,

"Jesus answered, "It is written: Man shall not live by bread alone, but by every word that comes from the mouth of God."

Jesus makes it clear one of the functions of the Word, is to feed humanity. He also demonstrates the power of the Word. In this statement, Satan was defeated, and the temptation left. See how powerful God's spoken Word is! It is life and it has authority over the devil and his works! In Matthew chapter 25, as Jesus describes the signs and events that will be in the future, he makes one more claim to the power of His words. Matthew 24:35:

"Heaven and earth will pass away, but my words will never pass away."

The power and authority within Jesus' spoken word is tremendous, full of life, and has creative powers. It is as powerful as what Almighty God used when He created earth.

It is even more powerful and full of life than the planet where humanity resides. Jesus intended his followers to use His words. The Holy Spirit inspired the writing of the Bible so Christians could have access to His words. The inspired word of God, the Bible, is full of life-giving nourishment for God's people. Jesus commanded His followers to go and preach the good news. Christians are to tell or speak Jesus' story and His words to one another. His people are to call on God using His words. Human spirit needs the nourishment from God's words. In II Timothy 3:16-17, when Paul is mentoring Timothy he states,

"[16]All scripture is God-breathed and is useful for teaching, rebuking, correcting and training in righteousness, [17]so that the servant of God may be thoroughly equipped for every good work."

Somehow, the present generation has belittled the power of God's words spoken by God's people. The books of the New Testament, beyond the four Gospels, clarified the importance of words and the connection to people's soul (mind/heart/will) body. Paul describes the power of God's word in Hebrews 4:12,

"For the word of God is alive and active. Sharper than any double-edged sword. It penetrates even to dividing soul and spirit, joints and marrow; it judges thoughts and attitudes of the heart."

The Holy Spirit inspired the words in the Bible, making them living words with this kind of power. It is Christians' best

SPEAKING TRUTH: THE WORD OF GOD

defense and greatest source of power and succor as they live on this earth. The power of the Word of God as revealed within the Bible is just as strong and valuable today as it was when it was first placed on paper.

Jesus agreed that spoken words have greater effect on us within our spirit than most think. When walking this world, the first time, Jesus applied this understanding of spoken word within the context of our understanding of willful disobedience to God. As recorded in the Book of Wisdom, Proverbs, the following was taught to Jewish children.

Proverbs 4:20–23,

"20My son, pay attention to what I say; turn your ear to my words. 21Do not let them out of your sight, keep them within your heart; 22for they are life to those who find them and health to one's whole body. 23Above all else, guard your heart, for everything you do flows from it."

The words described here are the recorded words of God. Health was an outcome of keeping all of God's words in their spirit. In Jewish tradition, unclean meant carrying transgressions against God within oneself. People who were unclean were ostracized from society until they could be declared clean by a priest. Jesus is emphasizing what comes from a person's heart and out of our mouths in words is more damaging than disease or what might spread disease. In Matthew 15:10-11 & 17-20 it states,

*"¹⁰Jesus called the crowd to him and said, "Listen and understand.
¹¹What goes into someone's mouth does not defile them, but what comes out
of their mouth, that is what defiles them."*

*"¹⁷Don't you see whatever enters the mouth goes into the stomach and then
out the body? ¹⁸But the things that come out of a person's mouth come
from the heart, and these defile them. ¹⁹For out of the heart come evil
thoughts-- murder, adultery, sexual immorality, theft, false testimony,
slander. ²⁰These are what defile a person; but eating with unwashed hands
does not defile them."*

Jesus is trying to teach people that what is said has
greater effect on a person spiritually, than what is done with the
physical body. Again, the spirit part of humanity is what lives
on after the physical body dies. The soul, (center for will-
thoughts-emotions) is a mediator between a person's physical
body and one's spiritual body. Decisions are made within the
soul to support one's self-centered focus or God surrendered
focus. A person's words reinforce these choices. As stated to
Satan by Jesus in his first temptation, people need nourishment
that only the Word of God can give. This nourishment feeds
the spirit. Jesus is drawing attention to the fact that one's spirit
feeds on what is proclaimed in this world. Whether it is Holy
Words from the Bible or negative words, such as shame and
blame filled confessions, it feeds and builds who a person is.
Defensive and aggressive words out of one's mouth, also affect
a person's spiritual growth. These are the types of words Jesus

is describing as evil thoughts fueled by unforgiveness, resentment and anger.

One of his disciples, James, fills in the details of this warning of Jesus. In chapter 3 of the book of James. In verses 3-4 James compares the tongue to a rudder on a ship, small but controlling the direction a ship turns or a bit in a horse's mouth that can control the whole animal's speed and direction. Next, James states in verses James 3:5-6,

"⁵Likewise, the tongue is a small part of the body, but it makes great boasts. Consider a great forest is set on fire by a small spark. ⁶The tongue is also a fire, a world of evil among the parts of the body. It corrupts the whole body, sets the whole course of one's life on fire, and is itself set on fire by hell."

People have a choice about how to speak. They can speak life by quoting God's Words or they can speak evil by focusing on negative words. By placing one's desires, wants, and needs above one's relationship with God, a person opens the door to a heart that can corrupt the whole person. Or a person can choose to do as Jesus did with Satan in the desert, and quote God's Word. This choice feeds one's spirit and brings God's protection to His people. It defeats the devil and all his works.

Unfortunately, the world has counterfeited the idea of overcoming negative talk with positive talk. The world's approach builds a person's sense of self-entitlement, relying on their own strengths and abilities to solve problems and create opportunities. The push to develop one's self esteem requires people to own and speak their abilities. This process reinforces a focus on self. Parents and adults who work with children are encouraged to "help make every child a winner." Though the concept of being positive with children is morally acceptable, some caution is advised. Overuse of the process leads children to view adults as unrealistic about the true nature of children and their selfish behaviors.

Some children view these adults as too naive, thus untrustworthy. When that child begins to feel guilt, remorse, and blame for actions that are not socially acceptable, sometimes trusting adults to speak truth and help does not happen. Two things can then blossom. One is the child buries the guilt, shame, and blame, thus not moving towards forgiveness. The hidden unforgiveness begins the paths explained in earlier chapters. It becomes a secret, hidden within, that undermines truth. Or second, the child can ignore the problem, building on individual strengths and focus on self. Here, a definition of self grows based on actions and achievements. Both of these outcomes move a person from God centered focus to self-centered focus. A corollary to this happens when negative behavior is glossed over and not examined. The process of building a sense of responsibility and holding oneself accountable for their actions does not occur.

Rather than feeding a child totally on self-esteem, developing an understanding of who they are in Jesus Christ helps balance their sense of guilt and shame as well as placing their strengths in perspective with life. Admitting mistakes, discussing them, and assigning appropriate consequences for scripturally unacceptable behavior creates a balance. Practicing forgiving others whom the child deems "bad" with an adult helps build the process of letting go and trusting God. Declaring who children are in relationship to Jesus Christ builds strength within their spirits.

God's Word

1. Carries the power of creation.

2. Defeats the devil and all his works.

3. Is alive.

4. Is so powerful it can cut through the spirit and soul and body.

5. Feeds a person's spirit.

6. Brings health to the physical body.

7. Is eternal, surpassing the life of the earth.

8. Weighs thoughts and attitudes of a person.

9. Is useful in training a person in righteousness.

So how does one follow Jesus' example of defeating the devil and his works by quoting the Bible? The process is simple. Claim truths God stated in the Bible out loud. This is called confessions of faith. Memorize some, so they are at a person's mind's edge to do battle when attacked by negative thoughts.

Below are some possible truth claims based on God's Word in the Bible. This is not a complete list. Find and create your own when reading in the Bible.

Source in Bible	Quotation	Statement
John Chapter 1 verse 12	Yet to all who did receive Him, to those who believed in His name, He gave the right to be children of God.	I am a child of God.
John chapter 15, verse 15	I no longer call you servants, because a servant does not know his master's business. Instead, I have called you friends, for everything that I	I am Jesus' friend

	have learned from my Father I have made known to you.	
Psalm 118 verse 6 & Romans chapter 8 verse 31	The Lord is with me; I will not be afraid. What can mere mortals do to me? What then shall be our response to this? If God is for us who can be against us?	God is on my side; I choose not to fear.
I Peter chapter 5 verse 7	Cast all your anxiety on Him because He cares for you.	God cares for me and I am no longer anxious. He is my provider.
Matthew chapter 5 verses 10-12	Blessed are those who are persecuted because of righteousness, for theirs is the Kingdom of heaven	I am being delivered from all persecution. I choose not to be offended.
II Corinthians Chapter 5	Therefore, if anyone is in Christ, he is a	I am a new creation in Christ.

verse 17	new creation; the old has gone and the new has come	
Romans chapter 8 verse 17	Now if we are children, then we are heirs and co-heirs with Christ, if we indeed we share in His sufferings in order that we may share in His Glory	I am co-heirs with Christ.
II Corinthians chapter 12 verse 9	My grace is sufficient for you, for my power is made perfect in weakness.	God's power goes beyond my strength, overcoming my weakness and solving situations His way.
Romans chapter 8 verse 28	And we know that in all things God works for the good of those who love Him, who have been called according to His purpose.	God loves me and His plans for me are good.
Matthew	And surely I am	I am never alone

chapter 28 verse 20b Hebrews chapter 13 verse 5b	with you always, to the very end of the age. The Lord said, "Never will I leave you; never will I forsake you.	
Luke chapter 10 verses 17-19	The seventy-two returned with joy and said, "Lord, even the demons submit to us in your name." Jesus replied, "I saw Satan fall like lightening from heaven. *I have given you authority to trample on snakes and scorpions and to overcome all the power of the enemy; nothing will harm you.*	In Jesus name, I have power over the devil and his works.
Philippians chapter 4 verse 13	I can do all this through Him who gives me strength.	I can do all things by Christ who strengthens me.

Galatians chapter 3 verses 13-14	Christ redeemed us from the curse of the Law (of sin and death) by becoming a curse for us, for it is written: "Cursed is everyone who is hung on a pole." He redeemed us in order that the blessing given to Abraham might come to the gentiles through Christ Jesus, so by faith we might receive the promise of the Spirit.	I am redeemed and free from anything of the devil.
Philippians chapter 4 verse 19	And my God will meet all your needs according to the riches of his glory in Christ Jesus.	God provides for all my needs.
Romans chapter 5 verse 1	Therefore, since we have been justified through faith, we have	I have peace with God.

	peace with God through our Lord Jesus Christ through whom we have gained access through faith into this grace in which we stand.	
Colossians Chapter 1 verse 13- 14	For He has rescued us from the dominion of darkness and brought us into the kingdom of the Son He loves, in whom we have redemption, the forgiveness of sins.	I am rescued and forgiven.
Romans chapter 8 verse 1-2	Therefore, there is now no condemnation for those who are in Christ Jesus, because through Christ Jesus the Law of the spirit of life set me free from	I am free and no one can condemnation in me.

	the law of sin and death.	
Romans chapter 8 verses 34	Who then is the one that condemns? No one. Christ Jesus who died-- more than that, who was raised to life--is sitting at the right hand of God and is also interceding for us.	Jesus Christ is my advocate and helps me.
Romans chapter 8 verse 38	For I am convinced that neither death nor life, neither angels nor demons, neither the present nor the future, nor any powers, neither height nor depth, nor anything else in all creation will be able to separate us from the love of God that is in	Nothing can separate or end God's love for me.

	Christ Jesus our Lord	
Philippians Chapter 1 verse 6	...being confident of this, that He who began a good work in you will carry it on to completion until the day of Christ Jesus.	I am confident that God will perfect me in His way and His time.
I John Chapter 4 verse 4	You, dear children, are from God and have overcome them, because the one that is in you is greater than the one who is in the world.	The one in me is greater than he who is in the world.
II Corinthians chapter 2 verse 14	But thanks be to God, who always leads us as captives in Christ's triumphal procession and uses us to spread the aroma of the knowledge of	God always triumphs and He leads me to victory through Christ.

	him everywhere.	
II Corinthians chapter 5 verse 21	God made Him who had no sin to be sin for us, so that in Him we might become the righteousness of God.	I am Christ's righteousness.
II Timothy chapter 1 verse 7	For the Spirit God gave us does not make us timid, but gives us power, love, and self-discipline.	I have a sound mind and power through the Holy Spirit within me.
I Corinthians chapter 6 verse 19 - 20	Do you not know that your bodies are temples of the Holy Spirit, who is in you, whom you have received from God? You are not your own; you were bought at a price. Therefore, honor God with your body.	My body is a temple for the Holy Spirit.

These confessions can also be considered as affirmations of who a person is. They are what God has promised to each person as a result of accepting Jesus Christ as Lord and Savior. This is not a definitive list. There are many more truths in God's Word that are full of life. Be creative and find some verses that meet your own needs when reading the Bible. Trust the Holy Spirit to help you in the process. As stated in II Timothy, all of scripture is alive, so search the Old Testament for truths as well as for personal affirmations defining what a new creation in Christ looks like.

9

Activating the Holy Spirit

Jesus spoke about the Holy Spirit in his last dialog with his disciples before his death. It is recorded in John's Gospel.

He begins by telling them, "If you love me" (John 14:15). Accepting Jesus as Lord and Savior is the beginning of a journey, not an end. As stated in the three levels to maintain harmony with God, loving God is in the first level. As noted earlier, it is seeking an intimate relationship with God. This meets what Jesus states in John 14:15,

"If you love me, you will obey what I command."

This love is demonstrated in obedience and gratitude. It leads to the second level of accepting Jesus Christ for all He is and all He has accomplished. This level also includes trusting who a person is in Jesus Christ. Christians are a new creation through Jesus. It is a willing dependency on Jesus that is embraced. This lifts individuals up into spiritual wisdom as they overcome soul mind centered thinking. At this level, gratitude and further submission into spiritual truth arises.

Now Jesus gives a promise to those who are in this deep relational second level of harmony as recorded in John 14:16,

"And I will ask the Father, and he will give you another advocate to help you and be with you forever."

An advocate is also a counselor, a teacher and mentor. He is someone to lead and direct a person in making choices. Notice Jesus states to his disciples, another advocate. Jesus served this role with them when he walked the earth. Our Lord God honors the gift He gave humanity to choose through an independent will. Providing a counselor is within the bounds of free will. The counselor will help those at the second level of harmony with God to be better informed about the choices they make. He will use events a person chooses to enter as teaching opportunities to make informed decisions. As recorded in John 14:17, Jesus describes how they will know this advocate,

"the Spirit of truth. The world cannot accept him, because it neither sees him nor knows him. But you know him, for he lives with you and will be in you."

The people caught in their soul understanding do not have the spiritual eyes to see the Holy Spirit. Soul mind understanding only seeks truth by what is known through the five senses. It is processed through past experiences. As stated earlier, many times these experiences are colored by incomplete information. Sometimes emotions have overruled objective information and clouded the conclusions. This darkness of the world blinds those who do not seek God. As stated in 2 Corinthians 4:4,

"The god of this age has blinded the minds of unbelievers, so that they cannot see the light of the gospel that displays the glory of Christ, who is the image of God."

Without seeking God, no one can know Him. "Knowing" is an intimate relationship with Father God. Jesus is again referring to His previous statement that when the disciples accept Jesus as the Son of God, they know God (John 14:9). By spending time with Jesus, under His teachings, the disciples have developed a relationship with Father God. Jesus connects the thoughts of doing the works of God through Jesus to the experiences the disciples have had. They were sent to drive out demons and heal the sick under the authority of Jesus (Luke 9:1–6, Matthew 10 1–15, Mark 6:7–13). This Spirit of Truth, the Holy Spirit was with them. They were successful.

The promise is the Holy Spirit will live within them when Jesus completes His tasks. The disciples knew the miracles of healing and throwing demons out of people as personal experiences they performed under the authority of Jesus. The had sensed the Glory of God as they submitted in their spirits and overcame their soul minds. This is operating in faith. Each one could remember the patterns within themselves, when they sensed the Glory of God, and they chose to rise in their spirits. Jesus is reminding them of this knowing. This promise of having the advocate living in them was outside of soul mind understanding. It can only be embraced in faith, as a spiritual event.

When Jesus Christ arose from the grave and entered the room where ten of the disciples were present, Jesus breathed the Holy Spirit upon them. John 20:21-23:

"²¹Again, Jesus said, "Peace be with you! As the Father has sent me, I am sending you." ²²And with that he breathed on them and said, "Receive the Holy Spirit. ²³If you forgive anyone's sins, their sins are forgiven; if you do not forgive them, they are not forgiven."

Now Jesus spends the next few weeks re-teaching his disciples and explaining all things to them, so they are prepared to enter their mission as sent ones. The resting of the Holy Spirit upon them, as a spiritual mantle, as described in the Old Testament as it rested on prophets, had been accomplished. Jesus breathed a similar covering on them. He did not pour into their spirits. This mantle of the Holy Spirit allowed them to partake the wisdom Jesus taught at a deeper level than before his crucifixion. Yet it was not enough to accomplish what

Jesus required of them as carriers of the Gospel to the world. In Luke 24:48–49, Jesus delivers them further instructions,

"⁴⁸You are witnesses of these things. ⁴⁹I am going to send you what my Father has promised; but stay in the city until you have been clothed with power from on high."

Notice Jesus tells them that what is promised, the indwelling of the Holy Spirit, has not occurred. Despite having the mantle breathed upon them, the Holy Spirit has not been poured into them. In the discourse in John chapters 14-16, Jesus describes that the comforter, the counselor, the Holy Spirit would be sent to them, so they were not alone. They were to wait before proceeding with their mission in Jerusalem. The promise would come. During Pentecost, through the wind and fire of the Holy Spirit, each disciple was engulfed with the Holy Spirit. They began speaking in other tongues, as sign to all that something had changed within them. With this power inside him, Peter is now bold enough to preach to the people of Jerusalem.

Further into the book of Acts, the first Gentiles were brought into closer relationship with God, by Peter. When Peter defended his actions to the brothers in Jerusalem, he told of the manifestation of speaking in tongues as the proof these people were indeed saved by the blood of Jesus, just like the Jews. Acts 11:15-17:

"[15]As I began to speak, the Holy Spirit came on them as he had come on us at the beginning. [16]Then I remembered what the Lord had said: 'John baptized with water, but you will be baptized with the Holy Spirit.' [17]So if God gave them the same gift, he gave us who believed in the Lord Jesus Christ, who was I to think that I could stand in God's way?"

In Acts 10:44-48, Peter, who was convicted by the Holy Spirit that dwelt within in him, stated to Cornelius's people, the first Gentiles to receive Jesus Christ as Lord,

"[44]While Peter was still speaking these words, the Holy Spirit came on all who heard the message. [45]The circumcised believers who had come with Peter were astonished that the gift of the Holy Spirit had been poured out even on Gentiles. [46]For they heard them speaking in tongues and praising God. [47]"Surely no one can stand in the way of their being baptized with water. They have received the Holy Spirit just as we have." [48]So he ordered that they be baptized in the name of Jesus Christ. Then they asked Peter to stay with them for a few days."

Father God chose to reverse the order of baptisms with the first group of Gentiles to enter the covenant with God by the blood of Jesus. In His wisdom, Father God used the gift of indwelling of the Holy Spirit, and its proof by speaking in new languages, to open the eyes of the Jewish believers both the ones in attendance with Peter and the ones in Jerusalem. Notice, there are two baptisms. Both serve God's purposes of equipping the believer with authority and power. Salvation is already in place with the confession of faith. By examining the

Bible in depth, more scriptures that support the baptism of the Holy Spirit as a necessary step in the life of the believer can be found.

Today, speaking in tongues as a result of the baptism of the Holy Spirit is called prayer language. Many use this language to gain spiritual understanding of what God is asking of individuals or to clarify intercessions. In a time of great tribulation described in the Book of Jude, the advice to the believer is to pray in the Holy Spirit. Jude 1:20–21:

"20But you, dear friends, by building yourselves up in your most holy faith and praying in the Holy Spirit, 21keep yourselves in God's love as you wait for the mercy of our Lord Jesus Christ to bring you to eternal life."

Jude is referring to praying in a "prayer language" as in the Holy Spirit or through the Holy Spirit. Praying in the Holy Spirit is allowing the Holy Spirit to combine with a person's spirit and speaking directly to God. It pulls a person out of the reference of the physical world and the limitations of one's soul mind understanding based on one's experiences. It is like a water pipe added to move around a blocked section within a water system going directly to the need. People who have experienced this, rest on what Paul describes in Romans 8:26-27,

"26In the same way, the Spirit helps us in our weakness. We do not know what we ought to pray for, but the Spirit himself intercedes for us through wordless groans. 27And he who searches our hearts knows the mind of the

Spirit, because the Spirit intercedes for God's people in accordance with the will of God."

Speaking the prayer language is a way to discern the will of God. Using the prayer language is connecting directly from spirit to spirit. As Christians mature and the relationship with Jesus Christ grows, they thirst for a closer understanding of scripture. Prayer language helps one's mind within a soul, which is being tamed by the spirit to determine deeper meaning in scripture.

Developing this gift requires greater faith and trust. The awakened spirit within the individual speaks heavenly language to the mind of the soul. Being present in the spiritual realm is interpreted by the soul mind. An awe and wonder of the experience create a knowing of this being familiar. A person operating at the second level of harmony with God already has a faith that experiences God. Through this faith, judgment and a critical attitude is blocked. A trust of the familiar builds faith to wait for further revelation. By bending the will in the soul, the soul practices yielding to the spirit. The soul mind eventually can interpret and understand what is being released from the spirit and act upon it. Over time these pathways begin to operate both ways. The requests and needs of individuals, as known in their soul minds and hearts, yields through heavenly language to form requests. The person trusts the spirit language is stating what is needed and desired in the earthly realm. As it is released, many times the spirit will sense an answer or direction needed to complete the intent of the prayer. Now the people act or speak what has been imparted by the Holy Spirit through their spirits into their soul minds. That is why Jesus stated these things to His disciples. He was preparing them to yield to the Holy Spirit speaking through their spirits.

Mathew 10:20

"for it will not be you speaking, but it is the Spirit of your Father speaking through you."

Mark 13:11

"Whenever you are arrested and brought to trial, do not worry beforehand about what to say. Just say whatever is given you at the time; for it is not you speaking, but the Holy Spirit."

Luke 12:11–12

"11When you are brought before synagogues, rulers and authorities, do not worry about how you will defend yourselves or what you will say, 12for the Holy Spirit will teach you at that time what you should say."

It is through this baptism of fire and spirit that the awakened spirit possesses a direct connection to the Holy Spirit. The Holy Spirit now resides within the person. Operating within both realms is a learning process, led by the Holy Spirit. The Holy Spirit is the promised counselor.

A Prayer to Submit to the Indwelling of the Holy Spirit:

Heavenly Father, at this moment I come to you. I thank You that by His most precious blood, Jesus Christ has redeemed me and made me righteous in Your sight. I pray that the Holy Spirit come upon me. Lord Jesus baptize me now with the fire of God in the Holy Spirit. I receive this baptism in the Holy Spirit by faith in Your Word. May the anointing, the Glory, and the power of the Holy Spirit come into me now. May I be empowered for service from this day forward. Thank You Lord Jesus, for baptizing me in Your Holy Spirit. Amen.

Let go of thinking and rest in the peace of God. Trust in faith that you have received the Holy Spirit. Breathe in and allow peace to encompass your heart, your mind, and your will. Rest in this peace. Now, open up deep within your soul, a sense of thanksgiving and gratitude for the Love of God. Don't think, just flow in it! Open your mouth, let peace flow as your breath moves out of your lungs and in again. Breathe in the peace. Breathe out the gratitude and love for God. Surrender any control to the peace. A prayer language will start to build in your consciousness. Just let it pass by and into your mouth. Focus your mind on how much Jesus loves you. Release whatever is coming out of your mouth without any restrictions. It will sound strange. Like a baby first speaking, it will not sound like others. Just let it ride, knowing the Holy Spirit will develop it over time. Now praise God in your own tongue   and   mind!

10

The Armor of Christ

Ephesians 6:12

"For our struggle is not against flesh and blood, but against the rulers, against the authorities, against the powers of this dark world and against the spiritual forces of evil from the heavenly realms."

People who have confessed Jesus as Lord and turned their wills over to him have denied the pull of the self-centered lifestyle. It is imperative they realize they have tools available to help in their spiritual struggles. Before turning their lives over to Jesus, people may not have realized they were in a spiritual struggle. Though some were aware of sin, resentment, and remorse, many truly did not know that hanging onto selfish concerns, protecting their own interests, providing for their own needs was out of sync in the spiritual world with Creator God. The person who accepted Jesus as the Christ, the Son of the living God, and the author of redemption, has weapons God has created to fight the darkness in this spiritual realm.

As stated earlier, words are powerful and reflect thoughts and emotions. The warning in James chapter three is real. As James states in 3:9–12,

⁹With the tongue we praise our Lord and Father, and with it we curse human beings, who have been made in God's likeness. ¹⁰Out of the same mouth come praise and cursing. My brothers and sisters, this should not be. ¹¹Can both fresh water and saltwater flow from the same spring? ¹²My brothers and sisters, can a fig tree bear olives, or a grapevine bear figs? Neither can a salt spring produce fresh water."

Within this scripture also is an imperative that aids Christians. The opposite of misusing words is using the living Word of God as defense and offense against the powers of darkness. It is the first answer Jesus gave in his recorded confrontation with Satan in the desert after his baptism (Matthew 4:4). Humanity not only lives by physical food for one's physical body but also by every word that comes from God into one's spirit. The warning is that negative words also impact the spirit and bring chaos and destruction. Since humanity is first spirit and returns to our spirit form upon physical death, feeding the spirit is essential to our life.

Choosing the living words of God nurtures and feeds the spirit bringing life.

When Christians recognize they are in a spiritual battle, they need to use the weapons Jesus has given them through his sacrifice on the cross. Once, when Jesus explained about the mystery behind His statement that He was the bread of life, the disciples grumbled. They were only hearing his statements in their soul mind understanding. Jesus responded to the stuck mindset in John 6:63,

"The spirit gives life; the flesh counts for nothing. The words I have spoken to you—they are full of the Spirit and life."

Christians are reminded again, their lives are on two planes, the spiritual and the physical. When they focus on the physical, in time and space, they can be overwhelmed by problems. This focus is soul mind level, not spiritual. When Christians remember Jesus' sacrifice and that He possesses all power and authority in both worlds, present problems lessen. It is a rising in faith that this remembrance has power. They remember Christians are not in this thing alone! They have the Holy Spirit to guide them and lead them in spiritual solutions. In a person's weakness Jesus is stronger. The grace he gives each person is greater than anything one encounters in the here and now. The truth can set believers free if they remind themselves of it.

Christians' first line of defense then, is the Word of God as given in the Bible. As mentioned before, believers are to meditate on the Word, and know the Word. They are to use it in their affirmations of who they are. God's people are to confess the Word when they are attacked by negative thoughts or in times of stress and anxiety. Remember to thank God for all the positive and good that comes into one's life too. An attitude of gratitude focuses on one's provider, God. It defeats everyday pride. In Ephesians chapter five, Paul emphasizes this understanding by using praise to center us on joy. As stated in Ephesians 5:19,

"...speaking to one another with psalms, hymns and songs from the Spirit. Sing and make music from your heart to the Lord, always giving thanks to God the Father for everything in the name of our Lord Jesus Christ."

When Christians acknowledge God as the provider, the source of all goodness, they honor God. Believers remind themselves who controls the spiritual realm and that they know who the victor is. Everyday stresses and struggles are placed in proper perspective to eternity.

Armor of God

Ephesians 6:13–18:

"[13]Therefore, put on the full armor of God, so that when the day of evil comes, you may stand your ground, and after you have done everything to stand. [14]Stand firm then, with the belt of truth buckled around your waist, with the breastplate of righteousness in place, [15]and with your feet

fitted with the readiness that comes from the gospel of peace. [16]In addition to all of this, take up the shield of faith, with which you can extinguish all the flaming arrows of the evil one. [17]Take the helmet of salvation and the sword of the spirit, which is the word of God. [18]And pray in the Spirit on all occasions with all kinds of prayers and requests."

Paul tells Christians whose armor it is. It is God's personal armor they are putting on. It belongs to him, Father God, just like Christians belong to him. Armor covers every vulnerable part of a person. Putting on God's armor is covering everything believers are, everything that is vulnerable and exposed in God's strength and protection. When Christians go into battle, who does the enemy see when the armor is covering a person? The first statement, in verse 13, prompts people to be prepared. In other words, to daily put on the armor, so it is a habit. Any soldier tells us they prepare ahead of battle for all contingencies. In the midst of battle, it is too late to learn a strategy, try out a new weapon, or a new method. God commands His people to stand firm against the prince of darkness.

Jesus has already won the war! Satan is conquered and Jesus has all authority and power in heaven, on earth, and under the earth. Unfortunately, Satan knows he can cheat, lie, intimidate, and manipulate people at the soul level until Jesus appears for the last time and claims earth. God reveals this is true from the book of Revelation. The prince of darkness is still using lies, delusions, guilt, and shame to twist people away from their inheritance in Jesus. This is why Christians must rise up into the spirit, where victory has already happened! Before believers can act as Jesus' hands, feet, heart, mind, and everything else, they are called to prepare to stand with victorious Jesus. These are spiritual battles fought interiorly against the devil and exteriorly in our society. Thank God Christians are only asked to stand up for Jesus. His people are asked to call upon our Lord, submit to Him and wait. The weapons God gives His people are spiritual, and they need to practice using them in their daily life. Through practice, these weapons are automatic responses to anything that enters one's life that is not blessed by God. In a believer's daily talk and walk with God, practicing acknowledging the truth of the armor prepares one for standing when God needs His people to stand.

Having a continual dialog with God throughout the day also strengthens one's relationship with God. By using scripture, praise, and thanksgiving as actions to answer daily stress and anxiety, Christians no longer treat God like some cosmic Santa Claus to answer one's special wishes. By reminding themselves of dependency on God first, by honoring God for what is valuable in one's lives, Christians enter into a conversation with God with the correct attitude. The rest of the verses explain how to do the preparation and standing.

Start each day by placing the helmet of salvation upon one's head. It is a daily reminder to a person's thought life that through the death and willing sacrifice of Jesus, believers can now approach God. It is not due to anything a person has done, but rather an acknowledgment of turning over a person's will to God. As it states in the Lord's Prayer, "thy kingdom come, thy will be done, on earth as it is in heaven". By putting on the helmet of salvation, a Christian is turning one's will over to God and placing oneself under God's authority. God's people capture every thought and emotion and turn it over to the scripture they have memorized. In this manner, they declare God's spiritual vision for the world may happen here on earth. It is a symbol of who a person serves. When believers practice capturing every thought, turning it over in the presence of God, to examine one's motives, one's relationship and talk with God changes. They no longer have the audacity to claim they are equal to Jesus/God/Holy Spirit.

Place the breastplate of righteousness on next. In Roman times this breastplate covered the heart and lungs. May it serve to constantly remind a Christian it is Jesus Christ's Righteousness one wears. It is a badge of humility. Not in a person's own righteousness can one protect oneself! It is to motivate a person, to pass on the forgiveness and acceptance God has bestowed on them. Now one's heart center, the seat of one's emotions, including the emotion of pride, is aware that all actions taken are dependent on Jesus' blood. As Paul states, (Ephesians 2:9) "so no man can boast". It is a reminder that each person has forgiveness and a new life based on Jesus' sacrifice. It is a weighty reminder to show compassion and forgiveness to others. Christians cannot stand in judgement of other people's actions or words. Everyone has fallen short of staying in perfect harmony with Father God. As Jesus stated, no one is good except God (Mark 10:18). God's people are all new creations in Christ. Each individual has talents and gifts God has given them. God loves diversity. As a soldier, each person is to walk with fellow Christians, depending on Jesus' strength and skills to face the enemy.

Place the belt of truth around one's middle. Belts were anchors to hold worldly needs when traveling. The truth, as stated in the Bible, is Jesus (John 14:6). He is the Word made flesh. God does not lie. Christians are to gird or surround themselves with this truth. On it, God's people can hang everything they need to carry with them in this world. Surround oneself with God's Words. Now everything one needs will be provided by God. God loves His people much more than their daily needs require. Trust in God's love and provision. Give thanks to God for providing daily provisions. Dedicate all one has to God, thus acknowledging the source of one's daily provision.

To stand in this rough world, Christians need to shoe their feet in something that can handle the wear and tear. God's people are to place the gospel of peace on their feet. Jesus stated in this world people will have trouble, but they are to take heart since he has overcome the world. Jesus promised his believers to give them a peace that surpasses their understanding (John 14:27). Christians can rest in that peace. They can surrender their cares to Jesus. Without worries and cares they rest in the knowledge and hope of Jesus. It allows them to envision life differently. This peace gives believers hope and courage when the world does not see anything hopeful. Christians are to stand on this peace, rest in Jesus' peace, know they are more than conquerors within Jesus finished works. The calmness within the storms of life is believers' when we walk in this peace.

Now that God's people are clad in the protection of God, they can take up the weapons of faith to do battle in this spiritual realm. The first is faith. Hebrews 11:1:

"Now faith is being sure of what we hope for, and certain of what we do not see."

It transcends the earthly and trusts in the spiritual realm above all else. Despite what one's eyes and other senses know, this hope is in something greater than earthly wisdom and knowledge. It becomes a person's shield against all the thoughts, emotions and actions that lead to chaos. It is trusting in the Creator and His promises. This is a Christian's shield. It is a person's first line of offense against the things that are grounded in the world. It is a believer's answer to humanity's wisdom as the ultimate authority. It is hope for something greater than what people are experiencing now. The enemy's only power is accessed through the soul level. Jesus has defeated the devil and all his works. As stated in Colossians, Jesus has authority and power over all that was created. Colossians 1:19–20:

"¹⁹For God was pleased to have all his fullness dwell in him, ²⁰and through him to reconcile to himself all things, whether things on earth or things in heaven, by making peace through his blood, shed on the cross."

Our belief is the first offensive weapon to the lies and illusions created in this plane of existence. As Christians use it to attack lies, manipulations, intimidations, and illusions, the shield grows brighter and stronger. The memory of success feeds a person's faith. There are badges of successful encounters welded to the shield. As Christians honor them in memory (testimonies), their power grows stronger for the next encounter.

Christians' second line of offense against the powers of darkness is the sword of truth, God's Word. It is so powerful that it created all things humanity knows. Jesus is this power incarnate. Jesus has given his people permission to use these words that God has placed in their hands. It will defeat the devil at every turn. Knowing who people are in Christ Jesus and calling upon that power in them, accesses the Holy Spirit. Using the words of God will move mountains. Jesus told us so in Matthew 17:20-21,

"²⁰He replied: "Because you have so little faith. Truly I tell you, if you have faith as small as a mustard seed, you can say to this mountain. Move from here to there, and it will move. ²¹Nothing will be impossible for you."
Christians' faith is in Jesus Christ the conqueror, not themselves. Their confidence is solely in Jesus Christ and His victory. Christians are more than conquerors when they take up these weapons of the spirit. So not only are God's people called to stand in this world and be ready to follow where God leads them, but if attacked they have all the tools necessary to fight and win every spiritual battle.

11

Living in Harmony with God

In the first chapter, it was mentioned that God seeks a personal relationship with humanity. Three responsibilities for people to be in a healthy, fulfilling relationship with God are:

1. Harmony in relationship with God.

2. Harmony with oneself and knowledge of who a person is in Christ Jesus.

3. Healthy fellowship with others.

Harmony in relationship with God has been described in the earlier chapters, as well as the process of achieving this harmony. Pitfalls and wrong turns people may take, and the results of those choices have been described. The second responsibility of knowing who a person is in Christ Jesus and how to maintain that harmony has also been depicted. It is only the third responsibility that has not been delineated in specific details. This third level of harmony is best achieved after completing the other two levels. God created humanity to be social and relational with one another. There are steps in building healthy relationship with others that are interwoven with the other two levels. This is God's intent. Much discussion was given as to how destructive self-centered choices quench the harmony with God and can create barriers with other people.

Ultimately, it is the individual choices people make daily that determine how they interact with others in harmony or disharmony. These choices are based on the choice of surrendering to God or leaning into self. There is a strong connection between being in harmony with God's ordained order for Creation and relationships with other people. John explains this in I John 3:16-20,

[16]This is how we know what love is: Jesus Christ laid down his life for us. And we ought to lay down our lives for our brothers and sisters. [17]If anyone has material possessions and sees his brother or sister in need but has no pity on them, how can the love of God be in that person? [18]Dear children, let not us love in words or speech but with actions and in truth. [19]This is how we know that we belong to the truth, and how we set our hearts at rest in his presence: [20]If our hearts condemn us, we know that God is greater that our hearts and he knows everything."

There is a reason the first responsibility is to God. The third responsibility, giving and providing for others in need, can be accomplished without acknowledging God for who He is or accepting Jesus. People choosing to function from self-concern can see the needs of others. Many can be selfless in their giving. Yet the process of functioning from self-focus can reinforce the idea of judging others who do not give as lacking. It also sets up the need for solving world situations in worldly, earth-centered terms. Many times, this desire to help centers on changing others, rather than changing self. Yes, good can be achieved from this approach for a time. The main problem is staying in the physical realm and not connecting or feeding the spiritual realm. It does not transcend the world and the powers of Satan. Self-focus is still rebellion to the order of the Creation. The warning listed earlier concerning the path of unforgiveness and resentment can still be entered without embracing the first of the harmonies.

On the other hand, those who have chosen God over self, have submitted to God's will and have sought Jesus in their lives. If they practice the things described above, using spiritual weapons to overcome the world through the power of God Himself, there will be a greater, long-lasting contribution to God's intended purpose for the earth. It still distills down to a choice. Does one choose God and His method of redemption of does one build up self?

Meditative Prayer based on
Ephesians chapter 6 verses 13-18

Dear Lord God:

As I go out today, place upon me the Helmet of Salvation. Form within my mind the image of the Christ who died and rose that I might be in communion with you. Capture each of my thoughts today, before I speak them and surround them with the wisdom that only comes from acknowledging your sacrifice in everything I do.

I place the Breastplate of Righteousness on my chest. May it serve to constantly remind me that it is in Your Righteousness, and not my own actions that I have forgiveness and acceptance. Help me be your heart to all with whom I may come in contact today. May the love of Christ shine through my actions so others may see Jesus, not me.

I place the Belt of Truth around me. May the truth of God, as expressed through Your word, the Bible, gird me. May it become my center in all actions I commit today.

I put my feet in the Peace that passes understanding, that I might walk in Your ways. I rest in this peace, knowing you go before me to clear a path for me. Help me bring this Peace to your people in this world.

I pick up the shield of Faith. For you are my comfort and my strength. I stand in the Gap to which you have called me, trusting in Your Righteousness. For the Battle is the Lord's. Christ Jesus has already overcome.

Finally, I pick up your Bible, the Holy Word, as my sword. May I always remember it cuts both ways. Help me to direct it towards me, as well as the principalities of darkness, so You, Christ Jesus, remain Supreme Commander of my soul. It is in Jesus' name I pray. Amen.

Bibliography

All Biblical quotes are from New International version of Bible, unless otherwise noted.

Chapter One

Vine's Complete Expository Dictionary. 1996. (Thomas Nelson Inc. Nashville Tennessee) New Testament Section: Topical Index; page 122.

Chapter Five

Peggy Joyce Ruth. Psalm 91. 2002 (God's Umbrella Protection Ministries Copyright 2002) page 36

Chapter Six

http://www.vocabulary.com/dictionary/worship
http://www.oxforddictionaries.com/us/definition/american_english/worship

Chapter Seven

Vine's Complete Expository Dictionary. 1996. (Thomas Nelson Inc. Nashville Tennessee Nashville Tennessee) Old Testament section page 201,
Leaf, Carolyn. 2009.
Who switched off My Brain? (Thomas Nelson Publishers.) Pages 20-21.

Chapter Eight

Vine's Complete Expository Dictionary 1996. (Thomas Nelson Inc. Nashville Tennessee) New Testament section, page 683 reference "Word"

Made in the USA
Middletown, DE
20 August 2021